NO NONSENSE

FLY FISHING GUIDEBOOKS

David
COMMUNICATIONS

Taylor Streit's No Nonsense

Guide To Fly Fishing
In New Mexico

A Quick, Clear Understanding of Fly Fishing
New Mexico's Finest
Rivers, Lakes and Reservoirs

Published by David Communications • 6171 Tollgate • Sisters, Oregon 97759

Acknowledgments

This is the first fly fishing guidebook to cover the major waters in the entire state of New Mexico. Many experts, who know nearly *everything* about this vast area, helped. My thanks to all.

Bob and Lee Widgren of Los Pinos Fly Shop in Albuquerque for their overview of New Mexico fly fishing. Paul Zimmerman, also of Los Pinos, who has tubed every lake in the state. My son Nick, for his untiring field research and fresh, accurate perceptions. Tom Taylor, publisher of *Fly Fishing the Texas Hill Country* for editing, advising and typing. He and his charming wife Judy also housed and protected me during the writing process. Photographer Dick Spas devoted time and energy beyond the call of duty. My brother Jackson Streit helped, having written the excellent *No Nonsense Guide to Colorado*. Tom Knopick and John Flick of Duranglers gave info on the San Juan River. Van Beacham, my Taos guide competition. Ed Adams of the Santa Fe Fly Fishing School, for north central information. Randy Keys of Cottonwood Meadows fly shop. Franklin Fernandez, El Rio Fly Shop, for Rio Embudo data. Brett Lewis, of Brett's Steak House in Red River, New Mexico, for facts and helping the quality of fly fishing in those parts. Marty Frentzel and Bill Dyroff of the *Albuquerque Journal* sports desk. Jack Woolley, Ezra, Tyler and the folks at Los Rios fly shop in Taos. Norm Mabie of The Anglers Nook, a shop famous for accurate information. John LaFitte and the Mesillia Valley Fly Fishers who supplied the latest on Rio Penasco. Sam Moore of El Paso for his information on the Gila. Ramon Carrillo for southern New Mexico lake information. My favorite daughter, Chelsea Dawn Streit, who would like to have her name in this book. Garrett VeneKlasen, excellent writer and guide in Angel Fire. Gifted writers Gene Berry, Deb Theodore, Linda Pritchard and Craig Martin (Craig's *Fly Fishing In Northern New Mexico* is a must read). New Mexico Game & Fish fisheries biologists and other employees for their enthusiastic cooperation. National Forest Service and BLM personnel for valuable information. Pedro Arancet, Argentina. Tracy McCallum, Taos. High Desert Angler in Santa Fe. Publisher David Banks who's been supportive and marvelous to work with and has graciously allowed some digressions and thoughts on conservation. Special thanks to Rex Johnson and Ron Smorynski who confided their vast knowledge of Gila waters. Look for their book on fly fishing southern New Mexico.

Proofreaders and indispensable providers up-to-the minute facts and figures: Craig Martin, Paul at Los Pinos Fly Shop, Jack Wolley, John Lafitte, Norm Mabie, Ed Adams and Donna Banks.

Lastly, thanks to Mark Cowan, Jim, John and Scott Crowl, Keith Loveless, Larry Brown, John Biggers, Scott Drainey, Herb Dickerson, Leo Ortiz, Tom Simms, Mary Lou Palaski, Chuck and Felicia, Bill Leslie, Edwin Sasek, Eleanor and Phil Streit and all clients and friends and family who have helped me swim some pretty rough water and reach this more pleasant bend in the river.

Taylor Streit's No Nonsense Guide To Fly Fishing In New Mexico

©1996 David Communications
2,000 Improved & Updated Second Printing
ISBN #1-892469-04-9

Published by David Communications
6171 Tollgate • Sisters, Oregon 97759 • U.S.A.

Printed by Hignell Printing, Ltd.
488 Burnell Street, Winnipeg Manitoba, Canada R3G2B4

Author: Taylor Streit *Editor:* David Banks *Cover Design:* Pete Chadwell, Lynn Perrault
Maps & llustrations: Pete Chadwell *Front & Back Cover Photos:* Dick Spas

David Communications believes that in addition to local information and gear, fly fishers need fresh water and healthy fish. The publisher encourages preservation, improvement, conservation, enjoyment and understanding of our waters and their inhabitants. A good way to do this is to support organizations dedicated to these ideas.

David Communications is a member and sponsor of, and donor to Trout Unlimited, The Federation of Fly Fishers, Oregon Trout, California Trout, New Mexico Trout, Amigos Bravos, American Rivers, Waterfowl U.S.A., Ducks Unlimited, The International Game Fish Association, American Fly-Fishing Trade Association. We encourage you to get involved, learn more and to join such organizations. Trout Unlimited 1(800) 834-2419 • Federation of Fly Fishers (406) 585-7592 • Oregon Trout (503) 222-9091 • California Trout (415) 392-8887 • New Mexico Trout (505) 344-6363 • Amigos Bravos (505) 758-3874 • American Rivers (202) 547-6900 • Ducks Unlimited: (901) 758-3825 • IGFA (954) 941-3474 • AFFTA (360) 636-0708.

Disclaimer - While this guide will greatly help readers to fly fish,
it is not a substitute for caution, good judgement and the services of a qualified guide or outfitter.

This guide is dedicated to
Jim Brown, Richard Allen and Gene Berry

Stop this day and night with me and you shall possess the origin of all poems,
You shall possess the good of the earth and sun (there are millions of suns left),
You shall no longer take things at second or third hand, nor look through the
eyes of the dead, nor feed on the specters in books,
You shall not look through my eyes either, nor take things from me,
You shall listen to all sides and filter them from yourself....

I have heard what the talkers were talking, the talk of the beginning and the end,
But I do not talk of the beginning or the end.

There never was any more inception than there is now,
Nor any more youth or age than there is now,
And there will never be any more perfection than there is now,
Nor any more heaven or hell than there is now.

From *Song of Myself* - Walt Whitman

VICINITY MAP

REFERENCED STREAMS & LAKES

1. CIMARRON RIVER
2. EMBUDO DRAINAGE
3. GILA "WEST"
4. GILA RIVER
5. HIGH ALPINE LAKES
6. JEMEZ MOUNTAINS
7. JICARILLA LAKES
8. LOS PINOS/CRUCES BASIN
9. LOWER CHAMA RIVER
10. LOWER RIO GRANDE
11. MID-ELEVATION LAKES
12. PECOS RIVER
13. RED RIVER
14. RIO COSTILLA
15. RIO PEÑASCO
16. RIO VALLECITOS
17. SAN JUAN RIVER
18. TAOS AREA
19. UPPER CHAMA RIVER
20. UPPER RIO GRANDE

Contents

Acknowledgments iv
New Mexico Vicinity Map vi
Fly Fishing in New Mexico viii
The New Mexico
No Nonsense Fly-O-Matic ix
New Mexico Fly Fishing
Condition by the Month (Chart) xi
A No Nonsense Display of
Common Game Fish in New Mexico xii
A No Nonsense Display of
The Best Flies To Use In New Mexico xiii

Top New Mexico Fly Fishing Waters
Rio Chama, Upper Section 3
Rio Chama, Lower Sections 5
The Cimarron River 7
Rio Costilla 9
The Embudo Area 11
The Gila 13
The Gila "West" 15
High Alpine Lakes 17
Jemez Mountains 19
Jicarilla Lakes 21
Rio De Los Pinos 23
Mid Elevation Lakes 25
Pecos River 27
Rio Peñasco 29
Red River 31
Red River, Lower Section (Map) 32
Rio Grande, Upper River 35
Rio Grande, Lower River 37
San Juan River 39
Taos Area 41
Rio Vallecitos 43

Appendix
New Mexico Fly Tackle II
Additional New Mexico Information III
No Nonsense Fly Fishing Knots IV
Fly Fishing Terms VI
Other No Nonsense Fly Fishing Guidebooks VIII
Weigh Your Catch With A Tape Measure X
New Mexico Highway Map XII

Fly Fishing in New Mexico

Thoughts on the State, Conservation and the Future

New Mexico's license plates say it all. "The Land of Enchantment" has wondrous sights, sounds and attractions for everyone. New Mexico is home to unique Spanish and Native American cultures and life-styles ranging from the Santa Fe jet set to rural artists and cowboys. All live together under wild New Mexico skies and powerful vistas of mountain and mesa.

In New Mexico one can stay in a superb hotel, great B & B or camp deep in the mountains near the classical music of the trout stream. Many visitors learn about American Natives at places like Chaco Canyon, the Gila Cliff Dwellings or Taos Pueblo where people have lived continuously for 1,100 years. All this brings us to Argentina and yes, fly fishing.

I spend winter escorting fly fishers around beautiful Argentina (where it's summertime). Extensive trout fishing on those formidable rivers has helped me appreciate just how good New Mexico's fly fishing really is. The state isn't blessed with a great deal of water, but what there is can be very good. In short, fly fishing in New Mexico is varied and good, like the state's unique cultures, services and terrain.

New Mexico presents many fly fishing choices. They range from casting to big rainbows on the world famous San Juan River to fooling little native trout in remote wilderness creeks. If you prefer quiet fly fishing experiences, New Mexico has them. The extreme might be a horseback trip into the vast Gila Wilderness. You can fish the dry fly in small creeks and rivers and rarely see another human.

There are thousands of miles of these delicate waters in New Mexico. Only a few are mentioned in this guide. You'll have to discover your own special stretch, which is half the fun of this sport. In addition, we don't want a mad stampede that could harm the fisheries. Rather, a long period of discovery by intrepid fly fishers will help keep a lid on things. I hope you're one of these fortunate and considerate pioneers.

There is an obvious conflict in revealing special fishing spots. Fishing pressure may well increase with publicity, certainly a negative factor in a state such as New Mexico, where very little water is catch and release.

Many waters in New Mexico are protected by distance, rock, toil or sweat. Such remote areas, however, are also out of the public eye and mind making abuses more possible. I hope that more awareness and enjoyment of New Mexico's precious fly fishing resources results in discussion, action and protection.

Years ago, some of us protested as mining operations nearly killed fishing on the Red and Rio Grande. Our loud screams of warning seemed like whispers from out of the deep canyons. Now organizations such as Trout Unlimited, New Mexico Trout and Amigos Bravos are adding volume to a more consistent message of fish preservation and resource conservation.

In New Mexico, mining, grazing, logging, development and irrigation are adversely affecting water quality. Perhaps not as obvious to the casual observer, grazing in riparian zones is one of the most detrimental of these factors. Heavy hooves defoliate stream banks and slopes. Water temperatures increase and the effects of floods and droughts are exaggerated. Additionally, New Mexico is the only state without in-stream flow laws meaning that rivers can legally be sucked almost completely dry.

The good news is that New Mexico still has plenty of unspoiled country. It's our's to enjoy wisely and pass on to our children. Let's hope that we don't share the plight of English author W. H. Hudson. In his book *Far Way and Long Ago*, he laments the much changed Argentine home water of his boyhood. "I am glad to think I shall never revisit them, cherishing to the end in my heart the image of a beauty which has vanished from Earth."

The New Mexico
No Nonsense Fly-O-Matic

A quick-start guide to basic and unique features of fly fishing in New Mexico
(Especially for the out-of-state-visitor.)

How do we take the mystery out of fly fishing in New Mexico? Truth is, most fly fishing situations can be handled with common sense. But as a cab driver in the Bahamas told me, "Common sense ain't common." Here's what you need to know to successfully fly fish the best waters in New Mexico.

Gamefish

New Mexico is primarily a trout state and that's the focus of this guidebook. Don't overlook other gamefish however: smallmouth, largemouth, striped and white bass, kokanee salmon, lake trout, walleye and pike. The Rio Grande has good winter pike fishing. Maxwell, Morgan and other lakes, (see mid-elevation section) have good largemouth bass populations.

Catch & Release

Since C&R waters are few in New Mexico, please voluntarily return your trout to the water. Hold them loosely, with wet hands, upside down to remove your barbless hook. Push it backwards from the bend of the hook. Don't hold the hook near the hook's eye. Release tools work well on small fish and increase fly life.

Weather

New Mexico fly fishing is generally good during fair weather but best on overcast and the rare drizzly day. It's often very good just before and during a passing cold front, but then lousy afterward (Except in warm weather). In late summer's wet season fly fishing is usually best following the afternoon rain shower.

Altitude

New Mexico is very high and very dry. Most trout fishing is done at over 5,000'. Beware of altitude sickness and exposure to intense sun. Drink lots of water (not from the streams), wear sun block and a hat. Always be prepared for nasty weather with a warm pullover or rain jacket. I'm continually amazed how blue sky mornings can turn into mean afternoons!

Hazards

Meeting one's demise in a flash flood, from a lightning strike or from the fangs of a New Mexico panther, bear or rattlesnake might be a glamorous way to go. This certainly gets notice. Mosquito bites, altitude sickness, sunburn, dehydration, hypothermia or "beaver fever" caused by Giardia are more likely hazards. Lightning is a problem in New Mexico that out of state people might not understand. Beware! If you are in it, get away from tall trees and put your fly rod on the ground.

Use caution driving lonely highways at night. Elk, horses and cows love rich roadside vegetation. Always slow down where forest meets road.

Much of New Mexico fishing is in big, rough and rocky country. Be realistic about your physical condition and balance. Several people break bones in the Rio Grande gorge yearly.

Auto break-ins are possible in New Mexico, especially rigs left unattended overnight. Consider this when packing for trips and choosing parking spots.

Small Streams

The most important factor here is trout spooking. Fish upstream with dry flies. Stay low, with the sun at your back (when possible) and use any available cover to break your outline. Try getting a drag-free float with a #14 attractor dry fly that's easy to see. If you don't get any strikes, you're either scaring the fish or it's the wrong time of day.

Small high elevation streams cool down at night. They usually fish best midday after the water has warmed and insects become active. This is also true for most tailwaters. Lakes and large rivers are far less predictable, but generally fish best during low-light periods

Flies & Their Use

Other than on the San Juan, trout in new Mexico are, generally, not very selective. Elk Hair Caddis or Parachute Adams, #14-20, fool most rising trout when a drag-free float goes OVER them. Blue-Winged Olive dries and midges (for slower water) cover most other rising trout situations. Look about for Stoneflies, spruce moths or grasshoppers. If you see them, use this larger imitation. Bigger flies bring up bigger fish, hook better and are easier for you and the trout to see. They also support a beadhead nymph tied 2 or 3' behind the dry. This is an absolutely deadly set up for shallow water. In water 2.5' deep or more, fish nymphs tied the regular way. In most cases in New Mexico, this should be fished upstream with a dead drift back downstream. Add or subtract weight as needed so that your fly is close to the bottom. Use a strike indicator and set the hook as fast as humanly possible when the indicator does *anything*. Hare's Ear #12-18 and Peacock Nymphs #8-14 work very well.

Fly fishers are usually more picky about flies than are trout. Your fly fishing abilities and the trout's appetite are more important. Always get the current info and flies from a local fly shop before heading to the water. A list is in the back of this guide.

Rods

For most New Mexico fly fishing, 4 and 5 weight rods, 8 - 9' suffice. For small streams (without wind) 2 & 3 weight rods, 7 - 9' are fine. On big windy lakes, big rivers and when using big flies or weight, 6 - 7 weight rods, 8 1/2 - 10' are helpful.

Reels

For New Mexican trout, a single-action fly reel suffices. Click & pawl or disc drag is up to you. The fish in large rivers, like the San Juan, and large lakes, like Stone, are bulkier. Disc-drag reels help put the brakes on them. Backing fills the spool and reduces kinking. It also gives the angler some confidence when a hooked fish runs to the next county. Reels should hold approximately 50 to 100 yards of 20lb. backing.

The New Mexico
No Nonsense Fly-O-Matic
- Continued -

Lines

A floating fly line is all that's needed for most trout fishing in New Mexico. A weight-forward line helps combat wind and covers distance. Use a double-taper line for precise, presentation casting. Sink-tip lines are more user friendly than full sinking lines. Use either when lake fishing, particularly in warm summer months when fish hold in deep water. The most common weight lines are 4 to 6. The color of line doesn't seem to make a tremendous difference.

Wading Gear

Most waters in New Mexico can be fished with stocking-foot, lightweight hippers (hip boots) and chest waders with felt-soled wading shoes. During the warm summer months, wet-wade using wading shoes or boots and neoprene socks. Neoprene waders are necessary for float tubing and fishing the San Juan

Private Fly Fishing Waters

New Mexico, like many states, has some excellent pay-for-fly-fishing opportunities. For fly fishing and catching, these arrangements are generally a good value. Their inclusion here, however, in no way implies an endorsement. Fee-fishing is a popular, time tested and growing way to enjoy fly fishing. Opportunities of this type in New Mexico bear mentioning in this guidebook.

Vermejo Park Ranch and the **Lodge at Chama** are the state's most expansive properties. These sporting retreats are top shelf in every respect. Both serve gourmet meals, offer other activities and provide lodging and fly fishing in big, wild country. Prices are up there with world class resorts.

Vermejo primarily offers lake fly fishing and some very good small streams. Excellent damsel fly hatches provide great dry fly fishing from Mid-June to August. The lakes at The Lodge at Chama are deep and don't fish well on top, but are loaded with 2-3 pound fish. Good catches are more than likely.

Rio Penasco Fishing Co. offers large platform wall tents and bath houses near a private spring creek. **Corkins Lodge** has a variety of cabins, a private lake and access to the Brazos River. **Twin Bell Lakes** are day use, catch and release stillwaters some 25 miles east of Albuquerque.

Guides

A qualified fly fishing guide will steer you towards the best fishing in places that match your ability, taste and condition. Your outing should include fly casting and fishing instruction. There isn't a New Mexico licensing system for guides but permits are required on BLM and Forest Service lands

Manners & Considerations

Use good judgement when fly fishing in New Mexico, or anywhere else for that manner. Here are the basics that apply in most situations.

- Abide by the laws.
- Respect private property.
- Don't litter.
- Never crowd another fisher.
- Catch and release.
- Support conservation groups.

Crowding

Urban dwellers (city folks) have a different idea of this than country folks. Generally there's lots of room on New Mexico fly fishing waters. This room is measured in miles, or parts thereof, like 3/4 mile, 1/2 mile, etc. Move away from others while they fish. And visitors, please acknowledge that your mannerisms, behaviors and values may be quite different from those of the area's residents.

Ratings

How do you rate a trout stream? What goes in the equation? Fishing pressure? Scenery? Solitude? Accessibility? The size and number of fish? I've tried to include all these aspects and more, when appropriate. For example, put fishing pressure in the equation for the San Juan River and it might not score very high. But on rivers like the San Juan you expect lots of people. My ratings take this into account. Or, hike miles up a remote river expecting solitude and fat cutthroats only to find screaming kids plunking worms to skinny browns and a low score might result. Expectations are a factor in the ratings, both in and out.

In this guide 0-5 is not worth writing about. A 6 is OK. A 7 is pretty good, an 8 good, a 9 is very good. The 10's I know of in New Mexico, are on private land.

Private Fly Fishing Waters in New Mexico			
Vermejo Park Ranch P.O. Drawer E Raton, NM 87740 (505) 445-3097	The Lodge At Chama P.O. Box 127 Chama, NM 87520 (505) 756-2133	Mulcock Ranch (Penasco River) 5299 Rio Penasco Road Mayhill, NM 88339 (505) 687-3352	Blackfire Fly Fishing Guest Ranch P.O. Box 981 Angel Fire, MN 87710 (505) 377-6870
Rio Penasco Fishing Co. 5365 Rio Penasco Road Hope, NM 88250 (505) 687-2143	Corkins Lodge P.O. Box 396 Chama, NM 87520 1(800) 548-7688	Brazos River Ranch P.O. Box 867 Las Vegas, NM 87701 (505) 425-1509	The Timbers At Chama (505) 588-7950 Twin Bell Lakes, Albuquerque (505) 766-9636

❖ x ❖

New Mexico Fly Fishing Condition by the Month

Here are general conditions for fly fishing waters in New Mexico by month. You can use this list to help plan your vacation to New Mexico. Or, if you are in the state, a quick glance at this chart will show you where to fish, given the time of the year. Always consult the local fly shops to get the latest information.

KEY
B: Best   **G**: Good   **F**: Fair   **P**: Poor   **N**: No fishing

	Jan	Feb	Mar	April	May	June	July	Aug	Sept	Oct	Nov	Dec
Cimarron	P	P	F	G	B	B	G	G	G	F	F	P
Chama (upper)	N	N	P	P	F	G	B	B	G	F	P	N
Chama (lower)[1]	F	F	G	B	G	F	P	F	F	G	B	G
Costilla[2]	N	N	P	P	F	F	B	B	G	F	P	N
Embudo	N	N	P	F	F	G	B	B	G	F	P	N
Gila	P	F	G	G	B	B	G	F	F	G	G	F
Gila (West)	P	P	G	G	B	B	G	G	G	G	F	P
Jemez	P	F	F	F	G	B	B	G	G	G	G	P
Jicarilla	N	N	P	F	B	B	G	G	G	B	G	F
Los Pinos	N	P	P	F	F	G	B	G	G	G	F	N
Pecos[3]	F	F	F	F	F	G	B	B	G	G	F	F
Rio Peñasco	G	G	G	B	B	G	G	F	G	B	B	G
Red River[4]	G	G	G	B	F	F	B	G	G	B	B	G
Rio Grande (upper)	P	F	F	F	P	F	G	F	G	B	B	P
Rio Grande (lower)	F	G	F	F	P	F	G	F	G	B	B	F
San Juan	G	G	G	G	G	B	B	B	B	B	B	G
Taos[5]	P	P	P	F	P	B	B	F	F	G	G	P
Vallecitos	N	P	P	F	P	B	B	G	G	G	F	P
High Lakes	N	N	N	N	P	B	B	G	G	F	P	N
Mid Elevation Lakes[6]	N	N	N	P	G	B	G	G	G	G	F	P

NOTES: All winter fishing is best during warm spells.

1 - For Chama below Abiquie dam. Below El Vado much colder weather in winter, flow rates very important.

2- Valle Vidal closed until July 1.

3 - At Villa Nuevo (good in winter).

4 - For Lower Red (Upper Red best from July 1 - October 1).

5 - For Lower Hondo and Rio Pueblo de Taos. Mountain waters are best from July 1 - Oct 1.

6 - For Northern lakes. Southern lakes fish better in winter.

A No Nonsense Display of
Common Game Fish in New Mexico

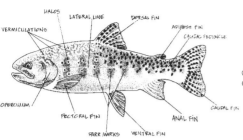

Typical salmon, trout or char. Most hatchery fish have a clipped adipose fin.

BROWN TROUT

Brown colored back with big black spots. Square tail and black and red spots on sides with light blue rings. Hard to catch, easily spooked.

RAINBOW TROUT

The most abundant wild and hatchery fish. An olive-bluish back with small black spots. Sides have light red or pink band. Lake 'bows' are often all silver.

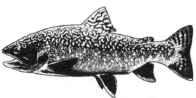

BROOK TROUT

'Brookies' are in the char family (Dolly Varden, Bull Trout, etc.). Back colors are black, blue-gray or green with mottled light colored markings. Sides have red spots with blue rings. Square tail. Lower fins are red and striped with black and white. Found in colder waters.

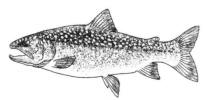

LAKE TROUT

In the char family (Dolly Varden, "Brookies" etc.). Back color is light-gray or green. White spots cover back and sides. Indented or split tail.

GILA TROUT

Dense pattern of small irregular spots and olive-green upper body. Sides shine gold with a pink band (adults). Cutthroat-type yellow mark under jaws. Fins tipped yellow and white. "Endangered with extinction" in N.M. Native to Gila River headwaters. Found in Leopold and Gila Wilderness. Apache trout (not shown), colored like Gila, without pink band and with denser spot pattern. Listed as "threatened". Found in Apache-Sitegraves N.F. and Ft. Apache Reservation.

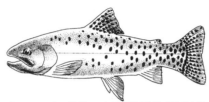

RIO GRANDE CUTTHROAT TROUT

Brownish green colored back, large black spots on tail decreasing in number towards head. Red-orange or rose colored on sides and pink or yellow underneath. Fins have orange tint, red or orange mark under jaws. Found in northern New Mexico, southern Colorado. Isolated populations in southern NM.

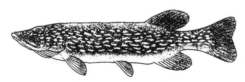

NORTHERN PIKE

Blue-ish to gray-green back with yellow to light gold spots in irregular rows. Long slender body, duck-billed snout and very sharp teeth.

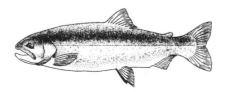

KOKANEE SALMON

Green-blue back with speckles. Sides and belly silver. Fall spawning turns color to dark red, leathery skin with green head. Male snout hooks and back humps, female body shape stays like trout.

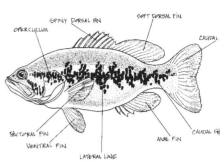

Typical bass, perch, crappie.

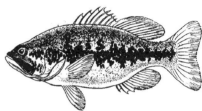

LARGEMOUTH BASS

Dark green back and sides with dark band o irregular spots along sides. Spiny dorsal fin (9-1 rays) separated from soft dorsal fin by deep notch Closed upper jaw extends to rear or beyond rear o eyes.

SMALLMOUTH BASS

Dark brown back with vertical bronze stripes on th sides. Spiny dorsal fin (9-10 spines) hasn't a dee notch separating the soft dorsal fin. Closed uppe jaw doesn't extend past the eyes.

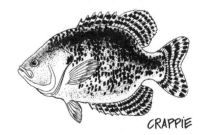

CRAPPIE

Silver and greenish with dark green or blac splotches on the sides. Compressed body wit upturned snout. Spines on dorsal, anal fins.

Illustrations by Pete Chadwell.

A No Nonsense Display of

The Best Flies To Use In New Mexico

These flies are available from fly shops, by mail or can be tied using the recipes.

Trout

Dry Patterns

Mothy (Taylor Streit)
Hook: 94840 Mustad, 5210 Tiemco, #10-12.
Thread: Cream.
Body: Lt. dun or cream. thick.
Hackle: Ginger, clipped under and on sides.
Wing: Very full, light elk hair.
Note: Imitates Spruce bud moth, looks like caddis.

Terminator (Ed Adams)
Hook: 5212 Tiemco, #8-14.
Thread: Tan.
Body: Orange, yellow dubbing.
Hackle: Grizzly, palmered.
Wings & Head: Deer hair tied Muddler style.

Fly Line Damsel (Taylor Streit)
Hook: 2487 Tiemco, #12.
Thread: 6/0, light color.
Body: Thin, light colored floating flyline. Extend over eye.
Thorax: White dubbing.
Hackle: Long grizzly, parachute style. Paint with blue magic marker.

Plopper (Taylor Streit)
Hook: 5212 Tiemco, #8-12.
Thread: Orange or Yellow.
Body: Long hollow dear hair in natural-tied colors. Tie lengthwise, folded over itself. Turkey, then deer overwing, Head Muddler style.

Ginger Dun (Franklin Fernandez)
Hook: 5210 Tiemco, 94840 Mustad, #12-16.
Tail: Straw colored ginger hackle.
Body: Ginger dubbing.
Wing: Upright Poly, cream.
Hackle: Straw colored ginger hackle.
Notes: For PM hatch on Embudo, Rio Pueblo deTaos Rivers.

Nymphs & Streamers

J.J. Special (Jim Jones)
Hook: 710C Dai-Riki, 75980 Mustad, #4-10.
Tail: Yellow marabou, copper Krystal flash, top with brown marabou.
Body: Brown chenille ribbed with copper crystal flash or tobacco brown sparkle chenille with gold tinsel.
Legs: 2 Yellow rubber legs each side.
Hackle: Grizzly palmered.
Notes: Southern NM lakes.

Olive Crystal Bugger (Taylor Streit)
Hook: 710C Dai-Riki, 75480 Mustad, #4-10.
Tail: Olive marabou, olive Krystal flash.
Body: Long flash (sparkle), olive chenille.
Hackle: Olive.
Notes: Best early season on lakes.

Dragon Slayer (Taylor Streit)
Hook: 9672 Mustad, #4-8.
Thread: Dark, 3/0.
Body: Olive Krystal chenille, over-wrap with hare's ear fur.
Hackle: Long Chuckar or mottled brown hen hackle.
Eyes, Head: Run 6 peacock across and clip.
Notes: Uglier the better.

Damsel Nymph (Taylor Streit)
Hook: 3906 Mustad, 3769 Tiemco, #12-14.
Thread: Olive, 6 or 8/0.
Tail: Olive mottled marabou, Krystal flash.
Body: Olive dubbing, Krystal flash rib-thin.
Thorax: Olive dubbing.
Hackle: Olive, 2 wraps.
Wingcase: Bronze, Peacock.
Eyes: Divide bronze peacock and clip.
Notes: Good deep or wiggled past rising fish.

Poundmeister (Taylor Streit)
Hook: 200R Tiemco, #6-10.
Thread: Dark, 3/0.
Body: Gray chenille, beaver fur overwrap, then add dam hackle, then lay 6 strands peacock herl over top.
Ribbing: Dun hackle. Over top 6-8 strands peacock, crystal flash rib after peacock is laid forward.
Head: Peacock.
Notes: Pain to tie, but effective.

Magic Midge (Mark Cowan)
Hook: #16-22.
Thread: Olive, black or brown, 8/0.
Tail: Strands of mallard flank.
Body: Thread.
Thorax: Black or dubbing to match natural.
Hackle: Grizzly, over thorax.
Wing Case: Dear hair clipped short but not flush.
Notes: Fish dry or just below surface.

ELK HAIR CADDIS

PARACHUTE ADAMS

MOTHY

BLUE WINGED OLIVE

ROYAL WULFF

MUDDLER MINNOW COPPER

PLOPPER

TERMINATOR

FLY LINE DAMSEL

GINGER DUN

PMD COMPARADUN

PEACOCK NYMPH

WOOLY BUGGER

J.J. SPECIAL

KRYSTAL BUGGER

DAMSEL NYMPH

HARE'S EAR NYMPH

MAGIC MIDGE

POUNDMEISTER

DRAGON SLAYER

Bass

WHITLOCK DEER HAIR POPPER

BLANTON WHISTLER

CLOUSER MINNOW DEEP WATER

Top New Mexico Fly Fishing Waters

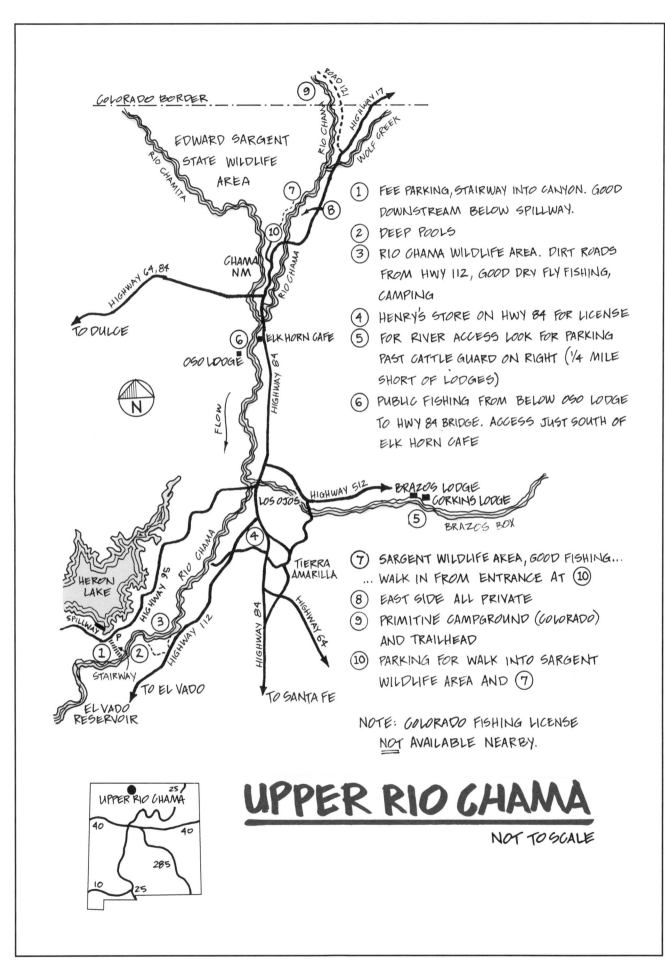

COLORADO BORDER

EDWARD SARGENT STATE WILDLIFE AREA

RIO CHAMITA

ROAD 121

RIO CHAMA

HIGHWAY 17

WOLF CREEK

⑨

⑦

⑧

⑩

CHAMA NM

RIO CHAMA

HIGHWAY 64, 84

TO DULCE

ELK HORN CAFE

⑥

OSO LODGE

HIGHWAY 84

N

FLOW

LOS OJOS

HIGHWAY 512

BRAZOS LODGE
CORKINS LODGE

⑤

BRAZOS BOX

HERON LAKE

HIGHWAY 95

RIO CHAMA

④

TIERRA AMARILLA

HIGHWAY 112

HIGHWAY 84

HIGHWAY 64

SPILLWAY

P

③

①

②

STAIRWAY

TO EL VADO

TO SANTA FE

EL VADO RESERVOIR

① FEE PARKING, STAIRWAY INTO CANYON. GOOD DOWNSTREAM BELOW SPILLWAY.

② DEEP POOLS

③ RIO CHAMA WILDLIFE AREA. DIRT ROADS FROM HWY 112, GOOD DRY FLY FISHING, CAMPING

④ HENRY'S STORE ON HWY 84 FOR LICENSE

⑤ FOR RIVER ACCESS LOOK FOR PARKING PAST CATTLE GUARD ON RIGHT (¼ MILE SHORT OF LODGES)

⑥ PUBLIC FISHING FROM BELOW OSO LODGE TO HWY 84 BRIDGE. ACCESS JUST SOUTH OF ELK HORN CAFE

⑦ SARGENT WILDLIFE AREA, GOOD FISHING...
... WALK IN FROM ENTRANCE AT ⑩

⑧ EAST SIDE ALL PRIVATE

⑨ PRIMITIVE CAMPGROUND (COLORADO) AND TRAILHEAD

⑩ PARKING FOR WALK INTO SARGENT WILDLIFE AREA AND ⑦

NOTE: COLORADO FISHING LICENSE NOT AVAILABLE NEARBY.

UPPER RIO CHAMA

25

40   40

285

10   25

UPPER RIO CHAMA

NOT TO SCALE

Rio Chama

- Upper Section -

The Chama is one of many fine rivers born in the vast snow fields of the San Juan Mountains. The Colorado portion of the river is without roads, unused and stunningly beautiful. Day fish from the campgrounds or dirt road, or backpack several miles upriver. Although I once wrestled a 24" female brown trout from this stretch, much smaller browns are what's common.

The New Mexico stretch of the Chama enters the state surrounded by private land. From Wolf Creek down, there's several miles of public water. Walk in from the west side of the river (#10) as the east side is also private. This unspoiled area offers excellent fishing and big fish. *Considerable* bushwhacking is required to reach the river, however, and it's rugged going once you get there. The region is rich in game and a run-in with a bear is quite possible!

Just down river from this area, the town of Chama provides a comfortable outpost. There's plenty of good food and lodging. Motels are often full, so call ahead. New Mexico Game & Fish maintains parking and access to the river just below town (#6). This dry-fly water is fished often, yet remains OK, especially just after runoff.

The Rio Brazos enters the Chama ten miles below town. It merits more coverage except it runs entirely through private land. New Mexico Game & Fish maintains access, however, just below the lodges. Walk down and fish your way back upstream with dry flies. Do this late in the day, as you'll have the sun at your back and the excellent caddis and mayfly evening hatches will be underway. Just upstream the river runs between the awesome Brazos Cliffs. Access to this rugged area is for guests of Corkins Lodge.

Farther downstream the Rio Chama Wildlife & Fishing area has special regulation water. Fly fishing this area requires moderate skill and energy and is an excellent destination for many. The Chama is larger here (50-70' across) but still fishes best with dries, or a hopper/dropper rig. Fish the deep pools, for 1-3 lb. rainbows, with nymphs.

Types of Fish
Rainbow, both wild and stocked and brown trout.

Known Hatches
Golden Stone, Stonefly, caddis, hoppers and Hendrickson. No hoppers on the Brazos.

Equipment to Use
Rods: 3-6 weight, 7 - 9'.
Reels: Mechanical or palm drag.
Line: Floating.
Leaders: 3x to 4x, 7 1/2 - 10'.
Wading: Hip, or chest waders in the slippery Brazos. Wet-wading in summer with felt-soled boots, especially on the Brazos.

Flies to Use
Dry Patterns: Golden Stones #8-12 (above town), Stones #14-16, Parachute Adams #12-18, Royal Wulff, Humpy #10-14 (Brazos), Dave's and Joe's Hopper, Stones #8-10, Plopper (1st choice below town) #8-12.
Nymphs: Hare's Ear (and beadhead), Pheasant Tail, Peacock, Prince #14-18.

When to Fish
After runoff, which is late in this area, usually July 1 to early-October. It can be cold in this area, dress in layers.

Seasons & Limits
Open year-around, except the Sargent Wildlife area: closed 2 weeks prior to Elk Season. Check regulations. Two fish limit in Sargent and Chama Wildlife areas.

Accommodations & Services
Chama has private RV parks, motels, market and gas. Public camping (tent) on upper river in Colorado, tables and toilets at Rio Chama Wildlife area.

Nearby Fly Fishing
Walk up Chamita creek, it's un-fished and may have beaver ponds. Also try Burns Lake by Parkview Hatchery and the Chama, below El Vado dam.

Rating
Plenty of decent 12-15" fish and generally little fishing pressure, overall an 8.

NOTE: THESE STREAMS ARE NOT SHOWN IN THEIR PROPER RELATIONSHIP TO EACH OTHER.

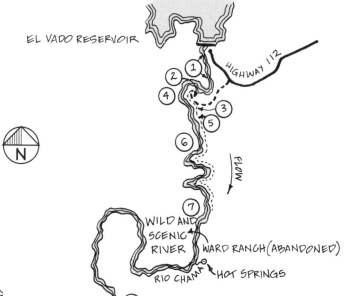

EL VADO RESERVOIR

HIGHWAY 112

FLOW

WILD AND SCENIC RIVER

WARD RANCH (ABANDONED)

RIO CHAMA   HOT SPRINGS

TO ABIQUIU RESERVOIR

N

TO EL VADO RESERVOIR

RIO CHAMA

ABIQUIU RESERVOIR

HIGHWAY 84

FLOW

HIGHWAY 96

PARKING

ROAD 162

RIO CHAMA

BELOW ABIQUIU RESERVOIR

1. STORE, GAS, LICENSE
2. OK FOR AUTO, PUBLIC LAND PAST BIG HOUSE
3. 4 × 4 NECESSARY HERE UP TO (7)
4. GOOD WATER
5. ENTER ROAD ON LEFT JUST AS ROAD CLIMBS AFTER MILE MARKER 216. LOOK FOR SECOND OPENING IN GUARDRAIL. USE CAUTION
6. CORNER POOL
7. FLAT WATER ABOVE, GOOD HOLE BELOW
8. FLAT WATER, PICNIC TABLES
9. GOOD ROAD, EASY ACCESS
10. ABIQUIU DAM AND ACCESS

BELOW EL VADO RESERVOIR

1. VERY GOOD, BROKEN WATER
2. PARK HERE & FISH UPRIVER
3. COOPER EL VADO RANCH... PARKING (SMALL FEE), CAMP, LODGING.
4. FOOTBRIDGE, WELL STOCKED
5. TRAIL
6. GOOD WATER THROUGHOUT
7. LONG WALK, GOOD FISHING!
8. APPROX. 20 MILES TO ABIQUIU RESERVOIR...WATER TOO WARM FOR TROUT.

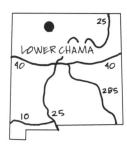

25

LOWER CHAMA

40   40

285

10   25

LOWER CHAMA

NOT TO SCALE

Rio Chama

- Lower Sections -

The two tailwaters of the Chama river are totally different from the free-running river above the dam at El Vado Reservoir. The curse of the upper Chama - low water - is what makes for good fishing below the dams. This must be qualified.

On both stretches, flow of under 300 CFS is necessary for good fly fishing. Fishing is even better at half that. In addition, the result of high flows during a wet decade was a general deterioration of the river, not to mention poor fly fishing. Compounding the problem are the flow demands of rafters (El Vado section) and irrigators (Abiquiu section). They are usually not in fly fishers best interest. It's best to call ahead for tailwater flows: El Vado (505) 758-8148 or (505) 262-5388, Abiquiu (800) 843-3029.

When conditions were very good (late 80's) the average fish below Abiquiu was 17" and there were loads of them. Construction and severe flash floods reduced the fishing at Abiquiu. It's still worth fishing, however, and may well return to its former glory.

Both tailwaters support tons of trout food. Fish tend to feed ferociously and then suddenly stop, especially at Abiquiu. One can go for hours without a single strike and then Bam! Bam! Bam!, one good one after another.

This is Woolly Bugger country. The water is usually murky and big, dark, flashy flies fished deep work well. Big brown trout sometimes move into very shallow water to feed, feeling safe because they can't be seen in the unclear water. The 20 lb. state record brown trout was caught below El Vado.

Though big hatches of caddis and mayflies occur, dry flies are seldom useful on these stretches. Along with Woolly Buggers, dead-drift nymph fishing works best. This often requires long casts. In either tailwater you need some fly fishing skill, a good guide, or preferably both.

Type of Fish
Rainbow and brown trout, 12-20". There's more fish at El Vado, though many are stockers.

Known Hatches
Caddis, various mayflies, hellgrammite (Abiquiu), cranefly larva, minnows.

Equipment to Use
Rods: 4-6 weight, 81/2 - 9'.
Reels: Big fish possible, disc drag is best.
Line: Floating. Sink-tip good for deep pools
Leaders: 2x - 4x, 9'.
Wading: El Vado is cold and treacherous, use chestwaders felt-soled boots and a wading staff. Abiquiu can be wet-waded in the hot season. Use waders at other times.

Flies to Use
Dry patterns: Elk Hair Caddis #14-18, Parachute Adams, Hoppers #12-20, plus various dries for different hatches.

Wet Patterns: Black Woolly Bugger, Olive Crystal Bugger, Muddler Minnow #4-10, Peacock #8-14, Beadhead Hare's Ear #12-18, Poundmeister #8-10.

When to Fish
El Vado: May-November. Prime time is August - November, at 300 CFS or *less*.
Abiquiu: Year-round when flows are below 300 CFS.

Seasons & Limits
Year-round. Limits: El Vado 6 fish, Abiquiu 2 fish.

Accommodations & Services
Cooper's El Vado Ranch, in El Vado, has camping and lodging, parking $3. Chama, 20 miles north has gas, food and lodging as does the town of Abiquiu just down river from the lake.

Nearby Fly Fishing
In the El Vado area, try the Upper Chama.

Rating
At low flow, when everything clicks, fly fishing here is a 10. At high flow when nothing clicks it's a 0. This averages to a 5.

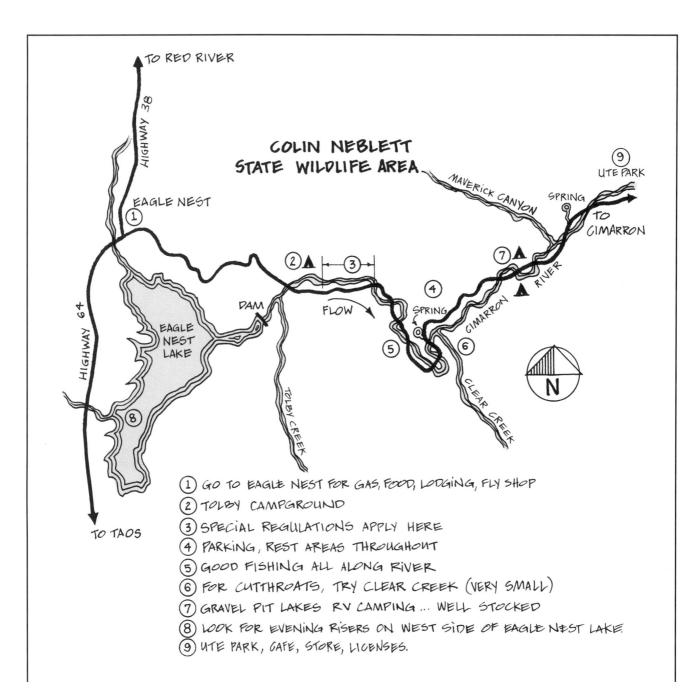

COLIN NEBLETT
STATE WILDLIFE AREA

① GO TO EAGLE NEST FOR GAS, FOOD, LODGING, FLY SHOP
② TOLBY CAMPGROUND
③ SPECIAL REGULATIONS APPLY HERE
④ PARKING, REST AREAS THROUGHOUT
⑤ GOOD FISHING ALL ALONG RIVER
⑥ FOR CUTTHROATS, TRY CLEAR CREEK (VERY SMALL)
⑦ GRAVEL PIT LAKES RV CAMPING ... WELL STOCKED
⑧ LOOK FOR EVENING RISERS ON WEST SIDE OF EAGLE NEST LAKE.
⑨ UTE PARK, CAFE, STORE, LICENSES.

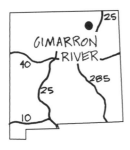

CIMARRON RIVER

NOT TO SCALE

The Cimarron River

Though seldom wider than 20', the Cimarron takes up a BIG space in the New Mexico fly fishing scene. It's a very popular tailwater fishery swarming with fat brown trout. It also fishes best when most other streams don't. That is, during spring runoff.

As a result, there can be (at times), lots of fishing pressure on the Cimarron. Happily, it never seems *too* crowded and one can find a little personal stretch to fish. Keep in mind good manners (and common sense).

The best tactic here is to slowly fish *up* the middle of the river. Fortunately, the water is often choppy and a bit murky, making it possible to get very close to the fish. And there are plenty. If you are not catching them they're probably not biting. Or, you're using the wrong fly, or it's hung up in the brush that lines the river. Look for spots your fly fishing skills can handle. Then roll cast, dab or do whatever it takes to get a few feet of drag-free float.

It's important to check flow rates of the Cimarron, since the river doesn't fish well when running full and up to the banks. Check Taos, Eagle Nest or Red River fly shops and the other sources listed in the back of this guide.

The special regulation section of the river (2 fish) has a gravel bottom, moderate flow and beaver ponds. Key on mayfly hatches here. Down river the water becomes faster and rockier and stone flies and caddisflies are more prevalent. These stretches are good dryfly water and, as in most tail waters, mid-day fishing is often the best. Stoneflies, PMD's and Baetis hatch routinely. Try to match the hatch on this river. Also, keep a low profile. The Cimarron runs due east, putting the late afternoon sun directly in your eyes, an advantage for the trout.

Regrettably (in my opinion), many of these trout are hatchery rainbows. I believe this decreases the overall number of trout available to the fly fisher. The stockers displace wild trout and don't survive the low winter flows as well as the wild browns.

Type of Fish
Brown trout, in the 10-14" range and stocked rainbows.

Known Hatches
May-June: Stoneflies, Golden Stone.
March-April: Blue- Winged Olive.
Summer: Pale Morning Dun.
Upper River: Green Drake, Midges.
Upper & Lower River: Caddis.

Equipment to Use
Rods: 2-5 weight, 7 - 9'.
Line: Floating.
Leaders: 4x to 5x, 7 1/2', longer in ponds.
Wading: Water runs cold. Wear chest-high waders and boots during high flows, otherwise hippers are OK. Wet-wading or hippers OK sometimes in summer.

Flies to Use
Dry Patterns: Stonefly with orange in body #8-10, Golden Stone #10-12, Quill Gordon (BWO) #16-20, Various PMD #16 (Comparadun fool 'em best, use parachute in fast water), March Brown, Ginger Dun #14-18, Green Drake #12-14, Parachute Adams #12-18, Elk Hair Caddis #14-18, Griffith's Gnat, Magic Midge #18-22, Midges #18-22 for slow water, Terminator #8-14.

Nymphs & Streamers: Woolly Bugger (black or green in high flows), Bird's Stone, Simulator #8-10, Golden Stone #10-12, Hare's Ear #14-20, Beadhead Hare's Ear #12-18, Pheasant Tail #14-20, Double Hackle Peacock #8-14, Olive Scud #14-16, Orange Scud #10-16.

When to Fish
March-October. Low water flows usually start in August, making fishing in the fall difficult.

Seasons & Limits
Fish year-round. From Tolby Camp Ground, 1 1/2 miles down river: 2 fish over 12", barbless hooks only. Always check current regulations.

Nearby Fly Fishing
When driving back to Taos or Angel Fire on a still evening, check the west side of Eagle Nest Lake for risers. Coyote Creek is a small but good stream 19 miles south of Angel Fire on Highway 434. This also fishes well in the spring.

Rating
If you *can't* keep your fly out of the brush, a 5. If you can, an 8.

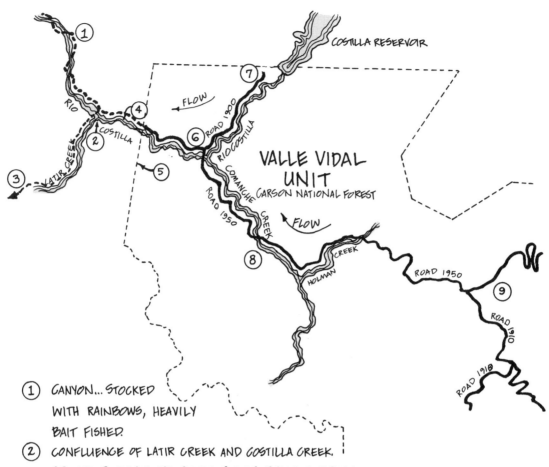

1. CANYON... STOCKED
   WITH RAINBOWS, HEAVILY
   BAIT FISHED.
2. CONFLUENCE OF LATIR CREEK AND COSTILLA CREEK.
   SPECIAL REGULATIONS START. SELF SERVICE CAMPING.
3. 4×4 ROAD TO LATIR LAKES... VERY ROUGH!
4. PARKING, OUTHOUSE, GOOD WATER.
5. BOUNDARY VALLE VIDAL UNIT
6. BRIDGE... VERY GOOD, BUT BRUSHY DOWN TO VALLE VIDAL
   BOUNDARY. UPSTREAM TO ⑦ MORE OPEN.
7. DEEP BEND POOLS, ROAD ENDS
8. COMANCHE CREEK GOOD ANYWHERE!
9. SHUREE PONDS, CAMPING

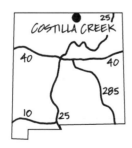

RIO COSTILLA

NOT TO SCALE

Rio Costilla

The Costilla is a tailwater, cutthroat trout fishery. It averages 20-25' wide and runs through a canyon and gorgeous high mountain meadows. The upper reach, in the Valle Vidal unit of the Carson National Forest, is managed for fish and wildlife including a marvelous elk herd. Although the excellent fishing is well known, the Costilla isn't very crowded. It's a long drive from just about anywhere.

Driving upriver, pass up the alluring waters in the canyon, because just above Latir Creek there's even better water and regulations. The river here runs through a treeless, easy-to-fish valley with a two fish limit. Farther upstream (see map, #5), in the lightly grazed Valle Vidal, the bare pastures of the lower valley give way to lush vegetation. This provides shelter for a lot of trout.

If you have the skill and patience, fish the tree-lined lower section of this valley. Trout here take a fly with assurance unlike in the open waters of the lower valley. In the lower section trout spit the fly out quickly. I sometimes tell clients to strike just before the take is expected. Then, just when you have your reflexes sharply tuned, a big Snake River Cutthroat will lazily drift up to inhale your fly and you'll snatch it away too soon. Keep at it.

When possible, fish two flies in the Costilla. Tie on a large dry fly with a small beadhead nymph trailing 18 -24" behind. Fish take the nymph 4 out of 5 times.

Little Comanche Creek is a wonderful dry fly stream, with small but feisty pure-strain Rio Grande cutthroats. It doesn't fish well when the water is low. It also fishes much better when the sun is off the water.

Types of Fish
Rio Grande cutthroats, pure and hybrids' 7-15", Snake River cutthroat 14-20", which occasionally wash over the dam and some rainbow, brook and brown trout.

Known Hatches
Golden Stone, stonefly, little green stone, some caddis, midges, PMD and Hendrickson.

Equipment to Use
Rods: 3-5 weight, 7 - 9'.
Reels: Mechanical or palm drag.
Line: Floating.
Leaders: 4x to 5x, 71/2 - 9'.
Wading: Hip, or chest waders. (It nearly always clouds up, rains or gets cooler in the afternoon here. Wet-wading gets questionable.)

Flies to Use
Dry Patterns: Stonefly #8-10, Golden Stone #10-12, Elk Hair Caddis #12-18, Parachute Adams, Royal Wulff #16-18, PMD #16, Hoppers #10-12, Gray Wulff, Terminator #14-18, Mothy #10-12.

Nymphs: Hare's Ear and Beadhead Hare's Ear, Pheasant Tail #14-18, Beadhead Prince, Zug Bug #14-16.

When to Fish
Friday noon through Sunday evening the water is low and best for fly fishing. During the week the flows are higher for irrigation. Good fishing is possible at high flows if you stick to edges and slower pools.

Seasons & Limits
Valle Vidal opens July 1. Catch and release on Costilla and Comanche Creek in Valle Vidal. Lower river (Latir Creek to Valle Vidal) the limit is 2 fish. In Shuree Ponds, the limit is 2 fish over 15".

Accommodations & Services
Some lodging at Ski Rio and the town of Costilla. Plenty of rooms, gas and food in Questa, Red River and Taos. License, gas, etc. in Amalia. Fee camping in Rio Costilla Park (505-586-0542) or in National Forest Campgrounds near Shuree Ponds.

Nearby Fly Fishing
Latir Creek and Lakes and Shuree ponds, where there is a kids only (under 12) water with huge fish!

Rating
If you strike fast, a 7.5 . If big Snake River cuts are washed over the dam at runoff, and you don't strike *too* fast on one, a 9.

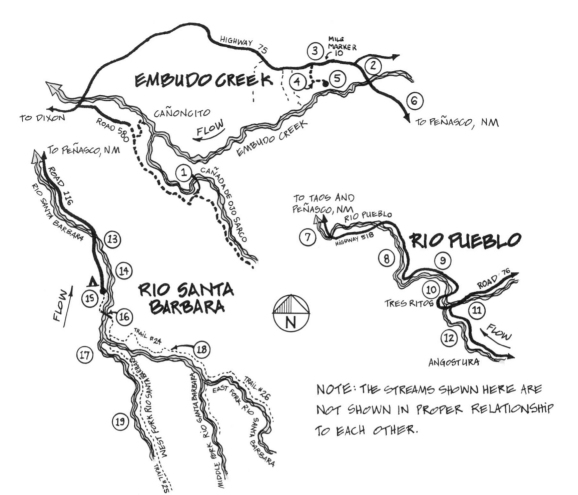

EMBUDO CREEK

1. SEE FACING PAGE FOR ACCESS DIRECTIONS
2. BRIDGE
3. 1.9 MILES FROM BRIDGE
4. PARK 2-WHEEL DRIVE HERE
5. PARK 4-WHEEL DRIVE HERE, FIND TRAIL AT END OF ROAD.
6. FLY SHOP

RIO PUEBLO

7. START CARSON NATIONAL FOREST
8. GOOD WATER HERE
9. GOOD FISHING HERE, ALSO
10. TRES RITOS... LODGING, GAS, FOOD, LICENSE
11. LA JUNTA CANYON... SOME CUTTHROAT TROUT
12. CREEK VERY SMALL HERE

RIO SANTA BARBARA

13. BRIDGE
14. BRUSHY, BUT GOOD
15. BUSY CAMPGROUND (FEE, AND TOILETS) PARKING AND CORRALS FOR PECOS WILDERNESS TRAVELLERS
16. FOOT BRIDGE, 2 MILE HIKE FROM CAMPGROUND
17. GOOD WATER, FISH UPRIVER
18. THICK FOLIAGE
19. MEADOWS... NICE

NOTE: THE STREAMS SHOWN HERE ARE NOT SHOWN IN PROPER RELATIONSHIP TO EACH OTHER.

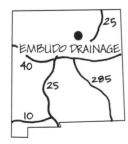

EMBUDO DRAINAGE

NOT TO SCALE

The Embudo Area

Like the nearby Taos and Red River areas, this drainage has three totally different streams. The Pueblo is highly accessible, heavily used and stocked. The Santa Barbara is in the high country requiring a walk to the fishing. The Embudo, formed by the meeting of the Pueblo and Santa Barbara, runs through a rugged and rather inaccessible canyon. These are interesting and popular places to fly fish.

The Rio Pueblo has many campgrounds, from primitive to modern and wheelchair-accessible fishing above Tres Ritos. Although fished with salmon eggs for the stocked rainbows, look for wild brown trout away from the large pools and obvious access points.

The Santa Barbara *can* have some great cutthroat and brown trout fishing. Some years back a client caught three, one pound, Rio Grande cutthroats in one pool. When I wrote about this gorgeous place in *Fly Fishing In Northern New Mexico* a few years ago, it was still pretty good. Now signs of overfishing are obvious, especially in the best pools in the West Fork meadow area. This area's delicate native cutthroat need total protection. Removing them makes it easier for the ever-encroaching brown trout to take their place.

Floods severely damaged the middle fork of the Santa Barbara. It's a tough river to fish in any case because of brush and deadfall.

The Embudo is canyon fishing. The two accesses noted on the map (see facing page) put you at either end of the canyon. Access #1: Just as road climbs away from tiny creek, look for turn off to left. Park. Climb road *on foot*. At top, follow trail north to river. Access #3 is easier only because one can drive part way. Between these two access points are several hard miles. Look for rattlesnakes, cholla cactus and brown trout. This is a gorgeous place to fly fish, however, with a few good (2 lb.) fish in the deeper pools.

As always, when fishing canyons, mark the trail and leave yourself plenty of daylight in which to get out. Bring a flashlight and matches in case you don't.

Types of Fish
Pueblo: Stocked rainbow trout, browns.
Santa Barbara: Stocked rainbow trout, browns., Rio Grande cutthroat.
Embudo: Rainbow and brown trout.

Known Hatches
Pueblo & Santa Barbara: Various mayflies, caddis, ants, beetles, and moths.
Embudo: Midges, caddis, Cream/Ginger mayfly, cranefly, minnows, ants, beetles, and moths.

Equipment to Use
Rods: 2 - 4 weight, 71/2 - 9', for dries on Pueblo and Santa Barbara. 4 - 5 weight, 8 - 9', for long casts on Embudo.
Reels: Mechanical or palm drag.
Line: Floating.
Leaders: 4x, 71/2' in Pueblo and Santa Barbara. 3x to 5x, 7 1/2-9' on Embudo.
Wading: It's slippery in Pueblo and Santa Barbara, use felt-soled hippers or chest-high neoprene with felt-soled boots. Wet-wade in the Embudo except in the fall.

Flies to Use
Dry Patterns
Pueblo & Santa Barbara: Attractor flies, especially Royal Wulff #12-16, ants and beetles .
Embudo: Ginger Dun #12-14 (for ginger mayfly hatch, most late-Spring and Summer evenings), Parachute Adams #12-18, Elk Hair Caddis #14-16, Hoppers, Black Body Humpy #8-12.

Nymphs
Pueblo, Santa Barbara: Beadhead Hare's Ear #14-16.
Embudo: Peacock #10-12, Poundmeister #8-10, Beadhead Hare's Ear #12-18, Prince #14-16.

When to Fish
Pueblo: June - October.
Santa Barbara: Best in midsummer.
Embudo: After spring runoff to November, except hot weather.

Seasons & Limits
Year around, no special regulations other than 2 cutthroat per day. Be sure things haven't changed and check Department of Game and Fish regulations or at a good fly shop.

Accommodations & Services
The town of Penasco has gas and groceries. Taos is close by for hotels and everything else.

Nearby Fly Fishing
Rio Grande, Rio del Medio and the Taos area.

Rating
As a rule these waters are heavily fished, so: Santa Barbara and Pueblo a 6, Embudo a 7.

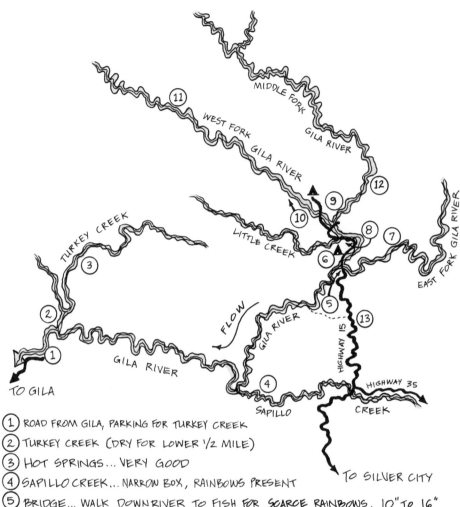

1. ROAD FROM GILA, PARKING FOR TURKEY CREEK
2. TURKEY CREEK (DRY FOR LOWER ½ MILE)
3. HOT SPRINGS... VERY GOOD
4. SAPILLO CREEK... NARROW BOX, RAINBOWS PRESENT
5. BRIDGE... WALK DOWN RIVER TO FISH FOR SCARCE RAINBOWS, 10" TO 16"
6. CAMPING, WITH OUTHOUSES
7. BIG FIRE IN UPPER RIVER IN '95. FISH KILLED IN
   LOWER RIVER. CHECK WITH FOREST SERVICE FOR ACCESS.
8. GILA HOT SPRINGS RV, GAS, STORE, OUTFITTERS, LODGING
9. VISITOR'S CENTER
10. GILA CLIFF DWELLINGS
11. WEST FORK - BROWNS IN UPPER RIVER, 'BOWS IN LOWER. GOOD UP A FEW MILES FROM CLIFF DWELLINGS
12. MORE TROUT UPRIVER. SMALLMOUTH IN LOWER SECTION.
13. ALUM TRAIL

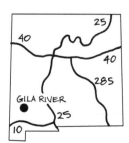

GILA RIVER

NOT TO SCALE

The Gila

There are better places to catch bigger trout. This is about getting way back in a perfect world and then going fly fishing — alone!

With 3.3 million acres of National Forest, nearly a third of it wilderness area, "The Gila" is music to the ears of outdoor lovers. It's big and wild. Enough so to have hidden the likes of Geronimo and the Hole in the Wall Gang. Famous hunter Ben Lilly found enough lion and bear to keep him happy. How solitary an experience is it today?

Gila fly fishing expert Rex Johnson has seen *one* other fly fisherman, in four years, while tramping 75 headwater streams in the area. Most streams are very small, usually with small fish. Sometimes, however, large trout 16" and larger are caught in these tiny streams in the big, deep undisturbed holes.

The main Gila (below the forks) is a lovely stream 40-50' wide. It's primarily a smallmouth bass fishery with awesome float fishing possible at the end of runoff. Day trips from Alum Trail or heading down from the bridge can be good but only in the deeper pools for smallmouth and the occasional rainbow.

The accessible water around the town of Gila Hot Springs gets summer and fall plants of rainbows. Fishing is better farther up the West and Middle forks and in the tributaries. This area is, as Aldo Leopold put it, "Too big for foot travel." A horseback trip with an outfitter is relaxing, but the best places (mostly rugged canyons) require lots of shoe leather. This area is also one of the homes of the endangered Gila trout, a situation that merits brief notice.

When other trout species were introduced to these waters, they crossbred and crowded out the natives. The Gila trout is now found in only a few protected headwater streams, closed to fishing. Over the years cattle grazing ruined river banks, raising water temperatures helping smallmouth bass to flourish. The bass are now displacing browns and rainbows, the early invaders. Ironically, native Gilas are tolerant of warm water, but now they're stuck "up a creek." Fortunately, grazing stocks have been reduced or eliminated in some areas. Though bad news for some ranchers, it's good news for trout and their friends.

Types of Fish
Brown and stocked rainbow trout, Gila/Rainbow hybrids and Smallmouth bass.

Known Hatches
Mayfly, caddis, hellgrammites, (stoneflies in cold tributaries), terrestrials, minnows, water boatmen (Gila).

Equipment to Use
Rods: 4 - 6 weight, 8 - 9'. Main Gila: 4 - 6 weight, 7 - 9'.
Reels: Palm drag is fine.
Line: Floating or sink tip.
Leaders: 3x to 4x, 7 1/2'. 2x, 9' for bass in lower Gila.
Wading: This is warm country, wet wading in boots is usually fine.

Flies to Use
Dry Patterns: For trout use attractors or Elk Hair Caddis, #12-16, hoppers, beetles, ants, moths, #10-14. Try a #10 Golden Stone in the Gila.
Wet Flies: Beadheads & Stoneflies #12-16 in deep pools, Gold Ribbed Hare's Ear #12-14, Olive Crystal Bugger #4-10.
Smallmouth bass: Yellow Marabou Muddler, Black or Olive Woolly Bugger, #4-8. Fish slow, deep water.

When to Fish
March - November. Lower Gila rafted in March and April during runoff. Allow a week to 10 days to backpack across the wilderness and you'll find plenty of places to fish.

Seasons & Limits
Fish year-round, 6 trout per day. Some areas closed for endangered Gila trout. Bass limit is 5 per day.

Accommodations & Services
Silver City (a very nice town), or Gila Hot Springs, has all services. Forest Service has a list of Gila outfitters.

Nearby Fly Fishing
Portions of Diamond and Beaver Creeks and Mimbres in The Black Range. Lake Roberts.

Rating
East Fork is a 0 because of fire and flood, but it will rebound. Lower Gila may have been affected, no rating. Upper Middle and West Fork, for scenery and solitude, a 10, for fly fishing a 7.

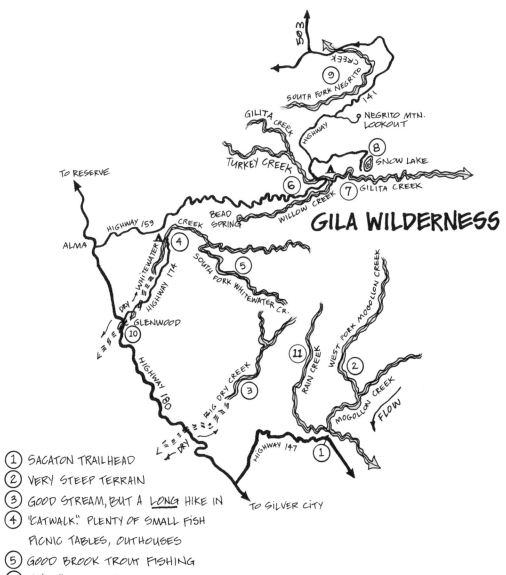

GILA WILDERNESS

① SACATON TRAILHEAD
② VERY STEEP TERRAIN
③ GOOD STREAM, BUT A LONG HIKE IN
④ "CATWALK." PLENTY OF SMALL FISH
   PICNIC TABLES, OUTHOUSES
⑤ GOOD BROOK TROUT FISHING
⑥ FAIR "DRIVE-BY" FISHING, LOTS OF SMALL FISH
⑦ 5 MILES OF SPECIAL REGULATIONS (2 FISH)
⑧ SNOW LAKE CAN BE GOOD. OUTHOUSES, WATER.
⑨ TRY HIKING IN FROM ROAD 503
⑩ GLENWOOD... NICE TOWN. STORE, LODGING, CAFE
⑪ SMALL NATIVES (GILA HYBRIDS)

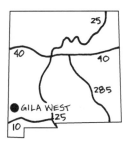

GILA WEST

NOT TO SCALE

The Gila "West"

Just north and west from the Gila River (previous pages) is another good area for "remote" fishing opportunities. To avoid confusion we call it Gila "West".

In an ever-shrinking natural world, a growing number of fly fishers find the surrounding arena as compelling as the fishing. Gila West is just this kind of place and exists as if still protected by the free Apache who ruled it not long ago.

Unlike the other Gila system's spacious river bottoms, the west side waters have steep, dark, narrow canyons that hold cold water. Even the north wood's brook trout are comfortable here. White-trunked Arizona sycamores and huge oaks shade the lower rivulets and their unique plant and animal life. Amazingly, life zones from Chihuahuan desert to Alpine forest lie within a few miles of each other here. There are several waters in this area about which I'll give brief comments and summaries.

The Catwalk over Whitewater Creek, where you can watch young wild trout feed, is more than a pleasant tourist attraction that's "fun for the whole family". This stream is rich with trout food and is a good place to catch wild trout. You may want to leave your rod in the car and go back for it later. Getting out of the car with the rod first thing has been known to upset some family members.

The South Fork of Whitewater Creek is also a good brook trout stream. Willow Creek is a popular camping and fishing area with stocked rainbow and many small brown trout (as is the Gilita). Such creeks are great for beginning fly fishers since catching any size trout is very encouraging.

Big Dry and Mogollon Creek (except the east fork, above the trail at Canyon Creek, which is closed) are apparently gorgeous and reported to have good fishing. They require great effort to reach. Plus Mogollon has protected Gila trout and is, as of now, closed to fishing. Farther north (40 miles) in remote Reserve, New Mexico there is fair fishing in Negrito Creek, but overgrazing is a problem in the area. Look for rocky canyons where livestock can't harm stream banks.

Types of Fish
Brown and Gila rainbow trout hybrids, brook and rainbow stockers in Willow Creek.

Known Hatches
Streams are small, insects are mostly terrestrial. Stonefly hatch in June.

Equipment to Use
Rods: 1 - 5 weight, 6 - 9'.
Reels: Palm drag is fine.
Line: Floating.
Leaders: 3x to 4x, 7 1/2'.
Wading: Wet-wade or use hip boots.

Flies to Use
Dry Patterns: Attractors, Elk Hair Caddis #12-16, Blue Dun, Blue-Winged Olive #14-16.
Nymphs: Beadheads for the deep pools.

When to Fish
March-November. July and August can be very hot. This is also the time for flash floods, which can be *very* dangerous in steep canyons.

Seasons & Limits
Fish year-around. Limits: 6 fish per day, 2 fish limit on the Gilita. Always check a current issue of New Mexico Game & Fish regulations.

Accommodations & Services
If taking Highway 159, start with a full tank of gas. Plan on camping everywhere. Silver City is the only large town anywhere near this area. Get as much information as possible by phone and mail from the Forest Service, New Mexico Game and Fish, and other sources (listed in the back of this guide) before venturing into the forest.

Nearby Fly Fishing
North on Highway 180 are several waters worth the trip. The villages of Reserve and Luna are your bases. Try Negrito, east of Reserve. The San Francisco river is 100 miles long and 30' wide and offers good fly fishing in "The Box", east of Luna and north of Reserve. Trout Creek, north of Luna, is fairly good, for small rainbows, according to reports. The San Francisco River, near Luna, is improving and fly fishing for rainbows at 7,000' can be good.

Rating
Drive to the fly fishing and it's a 5.5. The remote, hike-in fishing can be a pretty good, a 7.5.

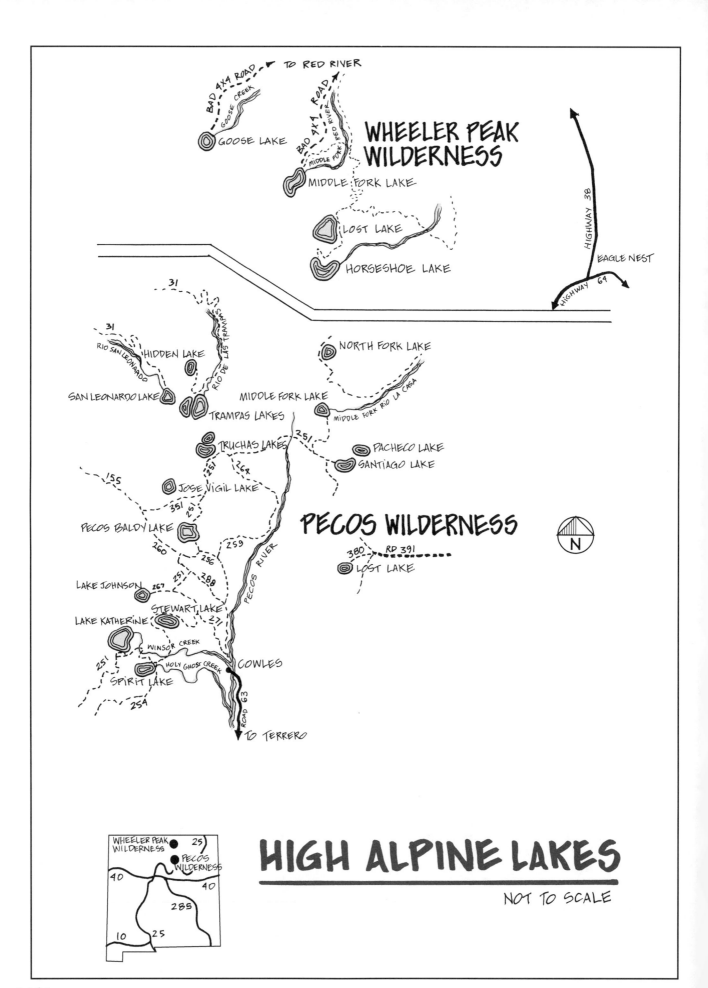

WHEELER PEAK WILDERNESS

TO RED RIVER

BAD 4X4 ROAD

GOOSE CREEK

GOOSE LAKE

BAD 4X4 ROAD

MIDDLE FORK RED RIVER

MIDDLE FORK LAKE

LOST LAKE

HORSESHOE LAKE

HIGHWAY 38

EAGLE NEST

HIGHWAY 64

31

31

RIO SAN LEONARDO

HIDDEN LAKE

RIO DE LAS TRAMPAS

NORTH FORK LAKE

SAN LEONARDO LAKE

TRAMPAS LAKES

MIDDLE FORK LAKE

MIDDLE FORK RIO LA CASA

TRUCHAS LAKES

251

PACHECO LAKE

SANTIAGO LAKE

155

JOSE VIGIL LAKE

251

264

PECOS WILDERNESS

351

251

PECOS BALDY LAKE

259

380   RD 391

260

256

LOST LAKE

PECOS RIVER

288

LAKE JOHNSON   267

251

STEWART LAKE

LAKE KATHERINE

271

WINSOR CREEK

251

HOLY GHOST CREEK   COWLES

SPIRIT LAKE

25A

ROAD 63

TO TERRERO

N

WHEELER PEAK WILDERNESS   25

PECOS WILDERNESS

40

40

285

10   25

HIGH ALPINE LAKES

NOT TO SCALE

High Alpine Lakes

Wheeler Peak & Pecos Wilderness Areas

Fly fishing in northern New Mexico's high country offers an experience to cast a fly amidst snow capped peaks, some over 13,000 feet in elevation. Numerous small lakes, nestled among the peaks, present the angler with sparkling cutthroat trout. Just being at this fascinating altitude can render fly fishing second to the magic of the high country. Approach these alpine lakes with this priority and you will not be disappointed.

We once hiked way in to a remote lake only to find it 95% frozen. Quite the disappointment until we found all the lake's trout massed in the 5% of open water. Though an unusually late ice-out (July 1) it shows how short the trout's growing season is at high elevations and why they tend to run small in size.

Happily, fly fishing high lakes is often done on top and to rising fish. Use a high-floating Elk Hair Caddis or Mothy with a midge (dry or wet) tied some 2' behind. Remember, when the large indicator fly swims off, somebody's got hold of the midge.

The other way to fish these lakes is to simply cast out a nymph or Woolly Bugger and strip in. Try floating line first, then go deeper with sinking or sink-tip lines.

Casting room can be a problem. Check topographical maps for treeless, gently sloping shorelines. On topo maps, treeless areas are shown white. Gently sloping shores have wider contour intervals. Call New Mexico Game & Fish for stocking information. This varies yearly and depends on winter-kill and other considerations.

Perhaps some of the exhilaration of this alpine experience is being in a foreign and sometimes unfriendly environment. For example, beware of lightening. I once took refuge in a ladies' outhouse (it was less offensive than the men's) during a furious a storm that dumped a foot of hail stones. Having been struck by lightening only a year before, I trembled while the lightening sizzled beneath the deafening thunder. When you travel above timber line, go early in the day before dangerous storms build.

Virtually all of these lakes require overnight backpacking or horseback trips. Be in shape. Pack and plan carefully. Use the maps on the left for *general directions only*. They are not to scale and should NOT be used for hiking or pack trips.

Types of Fish
Snake River cutthroat, 8-12" with 2 pounders possible. Some large cuts and rainbows are stocked in the Middle Fork of Red River and Goose Lake.

Known Hatches
Midge, moth, some Callibaetis and Damsel fly.

Equipment to Use
Rods: 4 - 6 weight, 8 - 91/2'.
Reels: Palm drag is fine.
Line: Floating, sinking tip, sinking.
Leaders: 5x, 9', for midges. 3x - 5x, 9' for bigger flies.

Flies to Use
Dry Patterns: Magic Midge - floating or under surface - Griffith's Gnat #18 -22, Parachute Adams #16-20, Elk Hair Caddis #14-16, Mothy #10-12, small attractors #16-18.

Wet Patterns: Midge larva (various), Kimball Midge, Peacock #10-14, Beadhead Hare's Ear, Zug Bug #14-18, Black Woolly Bugger #8-12.

When to Fish
The high country is usually snowbound until June. Fish right after May or June ice-out, until October.

Seasons & Limits
Year-round. 6 Fish per day, 2 cutthroat maximum.

Nearby Fly Fishing
Try any small stream in Pecos. Good fishing on the Upper Mora and Upper Pecos.

Accommodations & Services
You're limited to what's on your back and in your pockets. Better yet, what's on your horse's back and pockets. Goose and the Middle Fork of Red River Lakes are accessible by 4x4, but it's extremely rough going. There are jeep services in the town of Red River that can take you.

Rating
My brother Jackson summed High Alpine lakes well in the Colorado No Nonsense fly fishing guidebook: "The experience is always a 10."

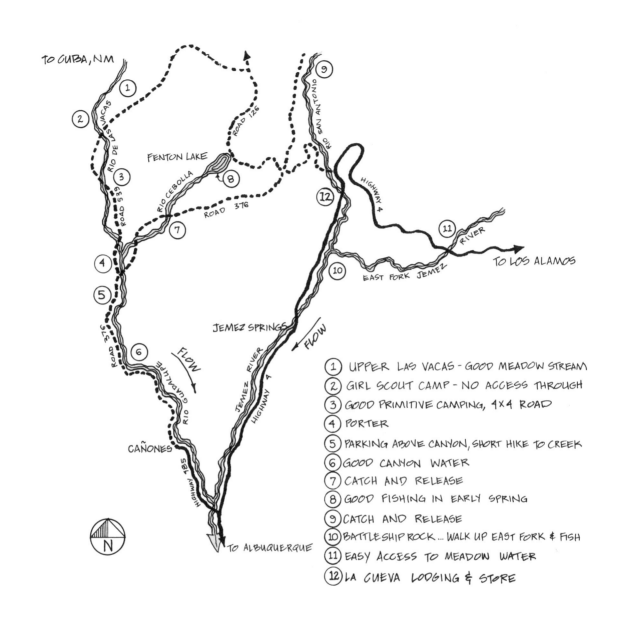

TO CUBA, NM

① UPPER LAS VACAS - GOOD MEADOW STREAM
② GIRL SCOUT CAMP - NO ACCESS THROUGH
③ GOOD PRIMITIVE CAMPING, 4×4 ROAD
④ PORTER
⑤ PARKING ABOVE CANYON, SHORT HIKE TO CREEK
⑥ GOOD CANYON WATER
⑦ CATCH AND RELEASE
⑧ GOOD FISHING IN EARLY SPRING
⑨ CATCH AND RELEASE
⑩ BATTLESHIP ROCK... WALK UP EAST FORK & FISH
⑪ EASY ACCESS TO MEADOW WATER
⑫ LA CUEVA LODGING & STORE

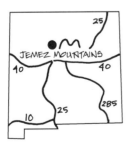

JEMEZ MOUNTAINS

NOT TO SCALE

Jemez Mountains

If one too many turquoise coyotes have howled at you in the streets of Santa Fe, put some classical music on, drive north and east through Los Alamos and go up into the Jemez. This gorgeous country, though close to major populations, has half a dozen fine fly fishing waters.

The area was created by an enormous volcanic eruption: a blast that sent boulders and ash into the Midwest. High peaks (over 11,000'), nutrient rich volcanic soil, forests and reasonably good access roads add up to one fine area. If you doubt me, read Craig Martin's chapter in *Fly Fishing In Northern New Mexico* for more detail. For a No Nonsense summary consider the following waters and suggestions.

I'm partial to meadow streams like the upper Rio de Las Vacas (above the girl's camp). It flows through slow pools and shallow beaver ponds. Fly fishing can be technical and tough here, especially with the clear water and skies of fall. Plan on a long drive to Las Vacas.

The Guadalupe is a canyon river, 20-30' wide. It has healthy but reclusive browns in the deeper pools. Try for them during the spring Stonefly hatch when they are less cautious.

The Cebolla is very small but offers interesting fly fishing. Undercut banks hold good fish in the catch-and release stretch. Land abuse in the past forced the stream into the earth and created high banks. Stalking pools is difficult. Keep a low profile as you sneak over the banks. Try to avoid traveling in the water. This rather heavily fished stream has a gravel bottom that fly fisher's boots can damage (not to mention cow's hooves).

The East Fork of the Jemez also has good fly fishing. You'll have to walk a ways for the best water and to avoid others. A good plan is to park and walk awhile before fishing.

Types of Fish
Mostly brown trout and stocked rainbows.

Known Hatches
Stonefly, Golden Stone, Blue Winged Olive, Pale Morning Dun, Red Quill, Trico, caddis, midge, cranefly and hoppers.

Equipment to Use
Rods: 2-5 weight, 7 - 9'.
Reels: Palm or mechanical drag.
Line: Floating.
Leaders: 4x to 6x, 7 1/2 - 9'.
Wading: Wet-wading is often possible in this relatively warm country. In cool weather, use hippers with felt-soled boots. Chest-high waders are best in the canyon waters of the Guadalupe.

Flies to Use
Dry Patterns: Stonefly #6-10, Terminator, Stimulator #8-12, Hopper or Plopper #8-10, Blue Winged Olive #16-18, Comparadun (on quiet water), Pale Morning Dun, Parachute Adams #12-18, Elk Hair Caddis #14-16, Light Cahill, Ginger Dun #10-12, Magic Midge, various attractors #14-18.

Nymphs: Various beadheads, Hare's Ear, Pheasant Tail, Poundmeister & Brooks Stone (in canyons), Bitch Creek, Green Rock Worm, Double Hackle Peacock #14-18.

When to Fish
Fish this area earlier and later than the high mountains to the north and east. Try after runoff, usually early May. July, August and the first half of September can be too warm for good fishing. If so, fish higher elevations. It gets good again from mid-September on into November.

Seasons & Limits
Fish all year, but consult the Game & Fish regulations to be sure. Stretches of the Guadalupe, Rio San Antonio and Cebolla (see map, #5 &#7) are catch and release.

Accommodations & Services
Lodging and cafe in La Cueva. Good primitive car camping below the girl's camp on Las Vacas and along the Cebolla (use 4x4 to get there). Other camp sites are available in the area.

Nearby Fly Fishing
Rio Frijoles in Bandelier National Monument is a small brook trout stream. Try Fenton Lake and the special regulation stretch of Rio San Antonio. Various area headwater creeks can be fun.

Rating
This rating would be higher, but for the fishing pressure. The area is uncrowded by Eastern standards. Avoid summer weekends and overall it's a 7.

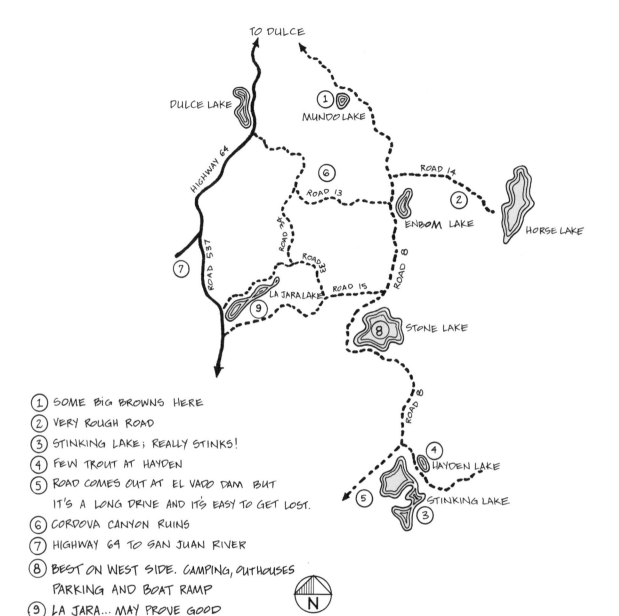

TO DULCE

DULCE LAKE

HIGHWAY 64

① MUNDO LAKE

⑥

ROAD 13

ROAD 14

② ENBOM LAKE

HORSE LAKE

ROAD 537

ROAD 34

ROAD 33

ROAD 15

⑦

⑨ LA JARA LAKE

ROAD 8

⑧ STONE LAKE

ROAD 8

④ HAYDEN LAKE

⑤ STINKING LAKE ③

① SOME BIG BROWNS HERE
② VERY ROUGH ROAD
③ STINKING LAKE; REALLY STINKS!
④ FEW TROUT AT HAYDEN
⑤ ROAD COMES OUT AT EL VADO DAM BUT
   IT'S A LONG DRIVE AND IT'S EASY TO GET LOST.
⑥ CORDOVA CANYON RUINS
⑦ HIGHWAY 64 TO SAN JUAN RIVER
⑧ BEST ON WEST SIDE. CAMPING, OUTHOUSES
   PARKING AND BOAT RAMP
⑨ LA JARA... MAY PROVE GOOD

N

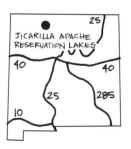

JICARILLA APACHE
RESERVATION LAKES

NOT TO SCALE

JICARILLA APACHE
RESERVATION LAKES
25
40   40
25   285
10

Jicarilla Lakes

The Jicarilla Apache lakes have long been known for their good trout fishing. Now, perhaps, the area contains New Mexico's best fly fishing lake available to the public. The million acre reservation is characterized by beautiful sandstone cliffs and spires that tower above Ponderosa pines.

Stone Lake was treated for trash fish in 1993. It was then stocked with rainbows who have grown rapidly in the competition-free water. Measured by length, girth, weight or between the eyes , these are studly fish: 2 - 4 pounds and up. Of course word about such fish gets around quickly. Expect a flotilla of float tubes and boats at Stone Lake. Well sheltered and not too big, all "Jic" lakes are good for tubing.

Stone is treeless and, on calm days when the fish are coming up, good dry fly fishing is possible when wading from shore. Otherwise, or 90% of the time, fish Stone with sinking lines behind boats (trolling speeds are all that's allowed) or from float tubes.

In 1995 La Jara Lake received treatment similar to Stone. If the improvements at Stone Lake are an indicator, La Jara could have excellent fly fishing soon. I don't believe Hayden or Mundo Lakes are worth much attention at this time.

If you like less company, try the lonely Horse or gorgeous Enbom Lakes. Fishing these is *usually* for that year's stocked fish (because of winter kill), but I've caught 3 lb. rainbows in Enbom. The fish in Horse Lake grow so fast that early season plants reach good size by late summer.

You'll see more people fishing at Dulce. Aerators in this lake help the fish survive the long winters. I've heard tales of great fishing just after ice-out.

If you've making an extended fly fishing trip and have yet to try fly fishing from a float tube, these lakes are a good place to start. Located about 1 1/2 hours from the San Juan, these lakes can be a pleasant change from the intense river fishing. Except for interruptions from big bothersome rainbows, your body, mind and soul are free to drift about the lake.

Types of Fish
Rainbow and some brown trout and cutthroat.

Known Hatches
Dragonfly, damselfly, Callibaetis and snails.

Equipment to Use
Rods: 5-7 weight, 8 - 10'.
Reels: Palm or mechanical drag.
Line: Full sink or sink tip, 10' +, medium rate or faster.
Leaders: 2x to 5x, 3' with sink tip lines.
Wading: Neoprene waders and fins for float tubes. Bank anglers use chest waders at Stone.

Flies to Use
Dry Patterns: Blue, Olive, Brown Damselfly, Parachute Adams, Elk Hair Caddis #14-16. Fish dries only when winds are low and fish are rising. Egg patterns early & late season at Stone.

Wet Patterns: Damsel #10-14, Dragon #6-10, Peacock #6-14, Black, Brown, Olive Woolly Bugger with crystal chenille, Beadhead Hare's Ear #12-16.

When to Fish
After ice-out, May - June and September - November.

Seasons & Limits
April 1 - November 30, 4 fish per day, 8 in possession, 2 fish at Stone Lake. No state license is required. Reasonable daily or yearly permit fees available in Dulce at the Game & Fish office, the Jicarilla Inn and other locations. Call Jicarilla Game & Fish, (505) 759-3255 for outlets and conditions. Stone Lake has a "one fly" rule. Note: Game & Fish regulations strictly enforced on reservation!

Accommodations & Services
Good hotel in Dulce, as well as groceries, gas, and air for tubes. Camping and restrooms at the lakes (except Horse). Air strip on the reservation.

Nearby Fly Fishing
Just north of Dulce is Navajo River — looks good but few fish seem to agree. San Juan is 1 1/2 hours west and Chama is 30 miles east.

Rating
Overall, an 8.

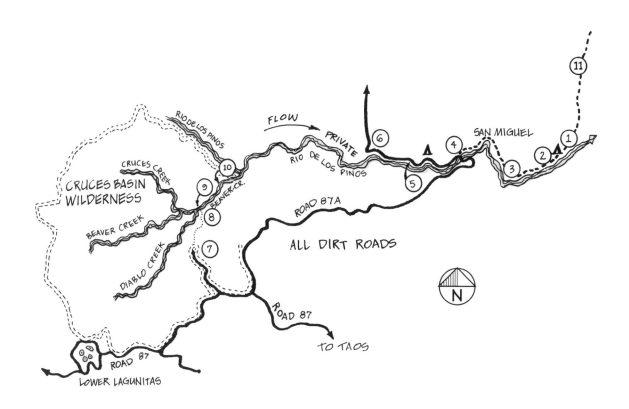

1. GOOD WATER, LOTS OF STOCKERS
2. CAMPING, TABLES, TOILETS, GRILLS THROUGHOUT
3. PRIVATE FROM HERE TO 4
4. BRIDGE... CARSON FOREST UPSTREAM, AND
   SPECIAL REGULATIONS
5. ROAD DETERIORATES, (MAYBE 4x4s ONLY) EASY WALKING
6. PRIVATE PROPERTY UPRIVER, GOOD WATER DOWNSTREAM, 4X4 ROAD
7. 9 MILES FROM BRIDGE AT 4, FAIR ROAD
8. MORE THAN 1 MILE FROM 7 & 300 OR 400 FOOT DROP
9. BEAVER PONDS
10. WATERFALLS
11. ACCESS FROM ANTONITO, COLORADO... 100 YARDS SOUTH OF HWY 285 & 17 JUNCTION. TAKE
    ROAD 125 THROUGH VILLAGE OF SAN ANTONIO, THEN TAKE GRAVEL ROAD HEADING WEST.
    FROM SOUTH ON HWY 285: TURN LEFT ON UNMARKED ROAD 2 MILES ABOVE STATE LINE,
    JUST BEFORE HWY 285 SIGN. CROSS BRIDGE AND TURN LEFT.

LOS PINOS/CRUCES BASIN

NOT TO SCALE

Rio De Los Pinos

- Cruces Basin Wilderness -

The New Mexico portion of the Los Pinos is an exceptionally pleasant and easy river to fly fish. Averaging 40' wide, this little gem of a stream has a gentle gradient and is seldom over waist deep. Perfect dry fly water. The river starts in southern Colorado, flows south and east parallel to the Cumbres & Toltec Scenic Railroad, then past Osier station and into New Mexico.

Although a long drive from anywhere, the river is fished regularly. Most fish are planted. They enjoy a rich insect diet and grow healthy and happy in short order. New regulations should help them reach decent size.

In 1995 special regulations (2 fish over 11") were placed on a stretch of water above San Miguel. Small browns were stocked. New Mexico Game & Fish and U.S.F.S. are considering ways to keep the trout from migrating elsewhere during low water.

If this zone sounds too tame, try the Cruces Basin Wilderness Area. Here you'll find a fine brook trout fishery, three creeks, water falls, beaver ponds and solitude.

If coming from Taos or Santa Fe and destined for the Cruces, take FS road 87 just south of San Antonio Mountain. It's a long, dusty ride, but gorgeous and remote. The walk to the creek starts at almost 10,000' elevation. The 1.5 mile descent to the water (300 or 400') takes less than an hour.

Fly fishing Cruces, Beaver and Diablo Creeks is similar: they're chock full of brookies up to 11". Bigger fish are possible in the beaver ponds below the forks. The creek then plunges straight down to the Rio de Los Pinos. It probably doesn't hurt to keep some 6-8" fish from this section. This gives other fish some elbow (or fin) room.

What does hurt are the biting flies in the area. I believe they're pals with the cattle roaming this "wilderness". Repellent works on neither. Letters to the Carson National Forest Service might, or wait until after mid-July when the flies depart.

Types of Fish
Los Pinos: Rainbow and brown trout.
Cruces Basin: Brookies.

Known Hatches
Golden Stone, Dark Stone, big brown & yellow mayfly, midges and caddis.

Equipment to Use
Rods: 3-5 weight, 7 1/2 - 9'.
Reels: Palm drag is fine.
Line: Floating.
Leaders: 4x, 7 1/2 - 9'.
Wading: Wet-wade in hot weather. Hippers OK in Los Pinos, waders are handy. In Cruces, hike in wading shoes then put on stocking foot hippers or wet-wade. Biting flies on Cruces until mid-July, wear long sleeves and pants.

Flies to Use
Dry Patterns
Los Pinos: Golden Stone #10-12, Elk Hair Caddis #12-18, Brown Wulff, Light Hendrickson #10-12, Stimulators #10-14, Parachute Adams #10-18.
Creeks: Attractors, Elk Hair Caddis, Parachute Adams #12-16.

Nymphs
Peacock #8-14 (smaller, late season), Hare's Ear, Pheasant Tail, Beadheads, Stonefly, Green Rock Worm #12-18.

When to Fish
Los Pinos: Mid-June to October, best early summer.
Creeks: Mid-June to September.

Seasons & Limits
Fish year-around. 2 Fish limit above San Miguel bridge. Consult New Mexico Game & Fish regulations.

Accommodations & Services
The towns of Antonito or Mogote, across the boarder in Colorado, have everything.

Nearby Fly Fishing
When these waters are low, the Conejos River (just north in Colorado) should fish well. Try the Los Pinos at Osier Station in Colorado. Ask directions and get a Colorado license at the fly shop in Mogote.

Rating
Los Pinos, improving with special regulations, a 7.5. Cruces Basin, for brook trout, an 8.5.

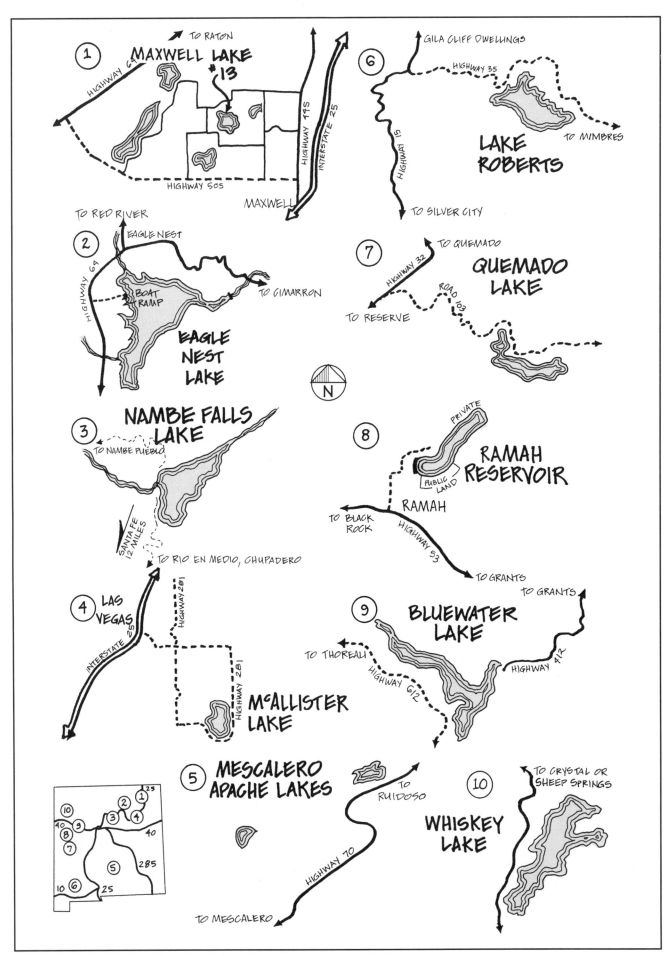

① MAXWELL LAKE #13

TO RATON

HIGHWAY 64

HIGHWAY 445

HIGHWAY 505

INTERSTATE 25

MAXWELL

② TO RED RIVER

EAGLE NEST

HIGHWAY 64

BOAT RAMP

TO CIMARRON

EAGLE NEST LAKE

③ NAMBE FALLS LAKE

TO NAMBE PUEBLO

SANTA FE 12 MILES

TO RIO EN MEDIO, CHUPADERO

④ LAS VEGAS

INTERSTATE 25

HIGHWAY 281

HIGHWAY 281

HIGHWAY 281

McALLISTER LAKE

⑤ MESCALERO APACHE LAKES

⑥ GILA CLIFF DWELLINGS

HIGHWAY 35

TO MIMBRES

LAKE ROBERTS

HIGHWAY 15

TO SILVER CITY

⑦ TO QUEMADO

HIGHWAY 32

QUEMADO LAKE

ROAD 103

TO RESERVE

⑧ PRIVATE

RAMAH RESERVOIR

PUBLIC LAND

RAMAH

TO BLACK ROCK

HIGHWAY 53

TO GRANTS

⑨ TO GRANTS

BLUEWATER LAKE

TO THOREAU

HIGHWAY 612

HIGHWAY 412

TO RUIDOSO

HIGHWAY 70

TO MESCALERO

⑩ TO CRYSTAL OR SHEEP SPRINGS

WHISKEY LAKE

N

25
①
②
③
④
⑩
40
⑨
⑧
⑦
40
285
⑤
10
⑥
25

Mid Elevation Lakes

Here are 10 stillwaters in New Mexico's 6,000 - 9,000' elevation range worth exploring with a fly rod. The others are often big, windswept and not suitable for the light rods and piddly craft we use. Although these lakes are popular with many home state flyrodders, most visits seem to prefer tumbling waters.

An advantage with these waters is that they often fish best when runoff in the mountain is in full swing and many rivers fish poorly or not at all. Lakes numbered 1, 4, 7, and 8 on the accompanying maps should be tops. Also, check the Jicarilla Lakes and private waters listed in this guide. Now, general observations about mid-elevation lakes.

Few lakes in the Rocky Mountains have natural trout reproduction. Many, such as Eagle Nest, get annual plants of millions of rainbow. These lakes also share similar characteristics such as elevation, amount of water, sunlight, vegetation, etc. Hence, they have similar food forms and are fished the same way. Fly rodding on these waters is done either from a boat or float tube, or from the shore.

In general, fish the hours around sunrise and just before dark. From boats, either troll very slowly, or drift with the wind. Travel in a straight line with 30-40' of line out. Try paralleling the lee shore in about 20' of water. Point your rod at the fly and don't set the hook until he's really on since fish often "nibble" before taking. *Use caution* in any small craft. Big seas can blow up quickly on these lakes. The wind is usually much lighter in the morning.

When fly fishing from a canoe or float tube observe the previous recommendations. I suggest resisting the urge to cast repeatedly. Trolling or drifting usually works best since more fish are available *in* the water than above it. Do cast to rising fish with Woolly Buggers. Fish shallow and close to shore early in the season. Go progressively deeper and farther from shore with sinking and sink-tip lines as the weather warms.

The following numbers and comments refer to the maps on the facing page: 1) Maxwell Lake #13, small, lightly fished, bass and nice trout. 2) Eagle Nest, try boat ramp area after ice-out. 3) Nambe Falls, small fee. 4) McAllister, very good early season for big fish. 5) Mescalero Apache, stocked heavily, no float tubes or boats. 6) Lake Roberts, dredging, other improvements may have helped. 7) Quemado, very good fishing early March or April. 8) Ramah Reservoir, trout and bass. 9) Bluewater, lots of water to cover, big lake. 10) Whiskey Lake, on Navajo Reservation, reportedly good. The best lakes for float tubes and bigger fish are 1, 4, 7, and 8. Use these maps for general reference only, *NOT FOR HIKING* or trail use.

Types of Fish
Rainbow trout. Largemouth bass in #1, 6, 8.

Known Hatches
Dragon and damsel fly, minnows, caddis, callibaetis mayfly.

Equipment to Use
Rods: 5-7 weight, 81/2 - 10'.
Reels: Palm or mechanical drag.
Line: Sink III (medium-fast sink rate), sink tips, floating.
Leaders: 2x - 3x leader with sinking lines, 3'.
Wading: Neoprene chest-high waders for float tubes or wear hippers for bank fishing.

Flies to Use
Dry Patterns: Blue Damsel #12, Elk Hair Caddis #12-16, Parachute Adams #14-16.
Nymphs: Dragon #610, Damsel #12, Black, Brown, Olive Crystal Woolly Bugger #4-10, Peacock (double hackles) #8-14, Beadhead Hare's Ear #12-16, Muddler #4-10.

When to Fish
After ice-out (varies) through spring. All waters fish slower in mid-summer. They get good again in the fall. Lake Roberts is good in winter, early and late in the day.

Seasons & Limits
Lake #13 and McAllister, March - October 31. Otherwise, fish year-around. Limit 6 fish on public waters.

Accommodations & Services
Most lakes have camping sites. Other services are often 1/2 to 1 hour drive away from each lake.

Nearby Fly Fishing
Little choice except Maxwell Lake (#13), Mescalero and Whisky have similar sized lakes close by.

Rating
Fly fishing varies greatly by day, lake and season. Generally in the ten waters listed it's a 7.5.

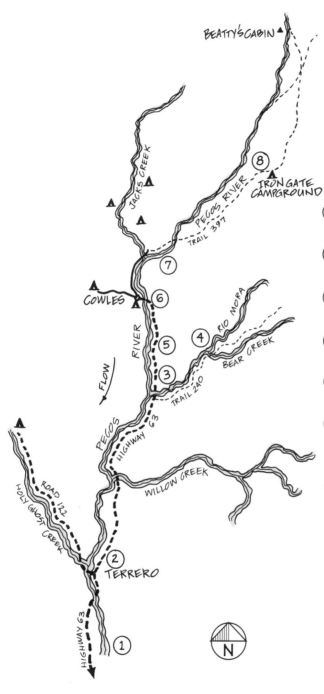

① SOUTH TO PECOS, ALTERNATES FROM PRIVATE TO PUBLIC WATER.

② WALK UPRIVER FROM STORE AT TERRERO FOR GOOD WATER.

③ PARK HERE, WALK UP TO ④ AND FISH RIO MORA. (OVER 1 MILE)

④ CONFLUENCE OF RIO MORA AND BEAR CREEK.

⑤ START SPECIAL REGULATIONS... FISH UPRIVER. (AKA. "THE BOX")

⑥ UPPER BOUNDARY FOR SPECIAL REGULATION WATER.

⑦ WALK UPRIVER A MILE OR TWO FOR BETTER FISHING.

⑧ TRAIL ABOVE IRON GATE LEADS TO THE RIO MORA MEADOWS AREA, IS LIGHTLY FISHED.

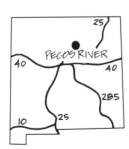

PECOS RIVER

NOT TO SCALE

Pecos River

The Pecos flows due south out of the gorgeous basin of the Pecos Wilderness area. Though only about 45 miles from Santa Fe, this forested watershed is nearly pristine. Trout are plentiful and fly fishing is consistently good. That's the good news. The bad news is, many people from nearby Santa Fe are aware of the good news. Certain fly fishing facts and tactics, however, can help overcome crowd problems on the Pecos. Most of this is common sense and applies to other popular waters.

First, realize a pod of parked cars does not mean fish are "running." It means the place is crowded and you need to find water away from easily accessed pools. Faster water draws less attention from fisher's and usually holds more *feeding* fish. In addition, indiscretions of presentation are less a problem in fast, riffled and broken water. Note: This is excellent water for a dry fly with a beadhead dropper tied on 18" behind.

The Pecos has a legendary Giant Stonefly hatch in late-May to June. Even the high waters of runoff can be great fishing with these bugs around. Work the slower edges of water where fish concentrate. These areas can be few and far apart in high water: check the inside of the river bends. Use extra caution if you wade the water during high flows.

Less crowded fishing on the Pecos can be found upstream above Jacks Creek. Years ago I backpacked into the Beatty's Cabin area. Using just one fly I caught dozens of "nonselective" browns. As the fly's feathers became skimpier, the hungry browns continued devouring the remaining shreds. Fly fishing is still good on the walk-in upper Pecos.

Types of Fish
Stocked rainbow, many brown trout, up to 16" possible.

Known Hatches
Giant & Golden Stonefly, some large mayflies, Baetis (Spring and Fall), midges, cranefly and caddis.

Equipment to Use
Rods: 3-6 weight, 7 to 9'.
Reels: Palm drag is fine.
Line: Floating.
Leaders: 4x - 5x, 7 1/2 to 9'.
Wading: This is a serious river during runoff — if you get in, chest-high neoprenes and a wading staff are essential. By July it's tamer and wet-wading is possible. Hippers good, chest-high waders best.

Flies to Use
Dry Patterns: Various Stoneflies (Birds, Terminator, etc.) #6-10, Elk Hair Caddis, Parachute Adams #12-18, Blue Winged Olive #18-20.

Attractors: Royal Wulff, Humpy, etc. #12-18.

Nymphs: Giant Stoneflies, Orange Golden Stone, Double Hackle Peacock, San Juan Worm, Egg patterns (for stocked rainbows in lower river), Hare's Ear, various beadheads #14-18.

When to Fish
June - October. Best mid-summer.

Seasons & Limits
Special regulations apply to "The Box" section and can change. Consult a current New Mexico Fishing Proclamation. Generally: Fish all year, 2 fish per day.

Accommodations & Services
Many campgrounds in the area, through they can be crowded on summer weekends. The Terrero store has licenses. Fly shops in Santa Fe.

Nearby Fly Fishing
Nothing nearby that's accessible by auto. The Pecos Wilderness is a great area for horseback riders or backpackers. The upper Pecos (above the falls) has "re-introduced" Rio Grande cuts. The upper Mora is good in the meadows and Bear Creek area. Many small creeks and high elevation lakes in the region are also good.

Rating
A 7.

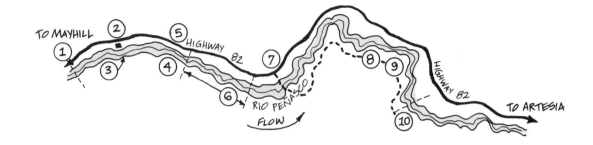

1. EASEMENT BOUNDARY, 12.7 MILES TO MAYHILL
2. ELK, (CONSISTS OF JUST A FEW BUILDINGS) PARKING, FISHING PERMIT BOX, FEE CAMPING
3. ACCESS TO RIVER, OK WATER BETWEEN ① AND ③
4. GOOD WATER HERE
5. RIVER ACCESS
6. PRIVATE PROPERTY
7. MULCOOK RANCH HEADQUARTERS. PARKING, PERMIT BOX
8. PARKING, 4 x 4 ROAD. WATER HERE IS NARROW AND DEEP, TOUGH TO FISH
9. HUT, PARKING FOR WATERFALLS AND GOOD WATER
10. EASEMENT BOUNDARY, 60 MILES TO ARTESIA (APPROX.)

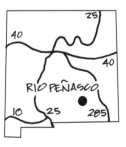

RIO PEÑASCO
NOT TO SCALE

Rio Peñasco

This is not a river one visits on a lark: unless you're heading for the beautiful White Sands National Monument or Carlsbad Caverns. The Peñasco is 66 miles from Mexico, just east of Alamogordo. It's probably New Mexico's best spring-fed trout stream.

It's hard to believe that good trout fishing is available so far down the map, at 5, 500' elevation and surrounded by desert country. The surprisingly large Mesilla Valley Fly Fishers in Las Cruces has helped make believers. The club deserves great credit for securing this private property, stocking fish, building protective fences and erecting signs and ladders. Please help them maintain this fine resource by following all rules and exercising fly fishing manners.

The fish I encountered (while wet-wading the Peñasco in December!) were not terribly spooky. I caught a few trout by simply strolling up and firing away. But if one fishes the Peñasco carefully, one can catch *more* than a few trout. Size up each pool, stay low, keep the sun behind you and use as few casts as possible.

The above experience was typical of the Bernard Cleves Ranch section. It fishes much like a regular freestone stream. Just below this section (#6 on map) additional springs create a more typical spring creek where water cress wave beneath a moderate current.

As of this second edition, the private section of river (see #6 on map) is accessible only through the Mulcock Ranch Peñasco River Fly Fishing Club (505) 687-3352, or the Rio Peñasco Fishing Co., (505) 687-2143.

One must be a member of Mesilla Valley Fly Fishers, Trout Unlimited or The Federation of Fly Fishers to fish on club property. You must also arrange to fish these leases before your arrival. I believe the fees are reasonable and the fly fishing worth the money.

To find out about permits contact the above or The Mesilla Valley Fly Fishers - P.O. Box 2222, Las Cruces, NM 88001. The Angler's Nook in Las Cruces, Los Piños Fly shop in Albuquerque, or High Desert Angler in Santa Fe can also provide more information. Norm Mabie at Angler's Nook usually has current conditions.

Types of Fish
Rainbow and brown trout, 12-20". Larger fish have been caught.

Known Hatches
Tricos, (plentiful except mid-winter) Baetis, (year-around) midges, caddis, scuds and hoppers (August-November).

Equipment to Use
Rods: 3-6 weight, 8 - 9'.
Reels: Palm drag is fine.
Line: Floating. Fast-sink near waterfall with Woolly Buggers.
Leaders: 2x to 3x, 9' with large flies in deep water. 5x, 9' for small dries and nymphs on flat water.
Wading: Wet-wading is usually OK. Lower water has mucky bottom.

Flies to Use
Dry Patterns: Tricos (tiny white wing) #16-24, Blue Winged Olive Compara Dun #16-20, Magic Midge #18-22, Tan Elk Hair Caddis #14-18, Parachute Adams #14-20, Dave's, Joe's, Plopper, Hopper #8-12.

Nymphs & Streamers: Beadhead Hare's Ear, Caddis #14-16, Tan, Olive Scud #16, Pheasant Tail #14-20 Wet Hoppers, #8-12, Olive, Black, Brown Woolly Bugger, #4-10, Poundmeister #8 (lower area), J.J. Special #6-8.

When to Fish
All year, mid-day in cool weather, early and late-day when hot. Upper Cleves Ranch can have very low water May-September.

Seasons & Limits
Year-around, state license required. On club lease and private waters usually 1 fish over 26". Brown trout caught in Bernard Cleve Ranch waters must be released.

Accommodations & Services
National Forest campground 2-3 miles west of Mayhill. Store, licenses, gas and motel in Mayhill. More lodging and cafes 30 miles west in Cloudcroft. Rio Peñasco Fishing Co. has stream-side lodging and guides.

Nearby Fly Fishing
In Ruidoso, NM, try the special regulation water (2 fish) on Rio Ruidoso. Look for parking just east of McDonald's near Chavez Excavating and Arby's.

Rating
A long way from anywhere, not free, but easily an 8.5.

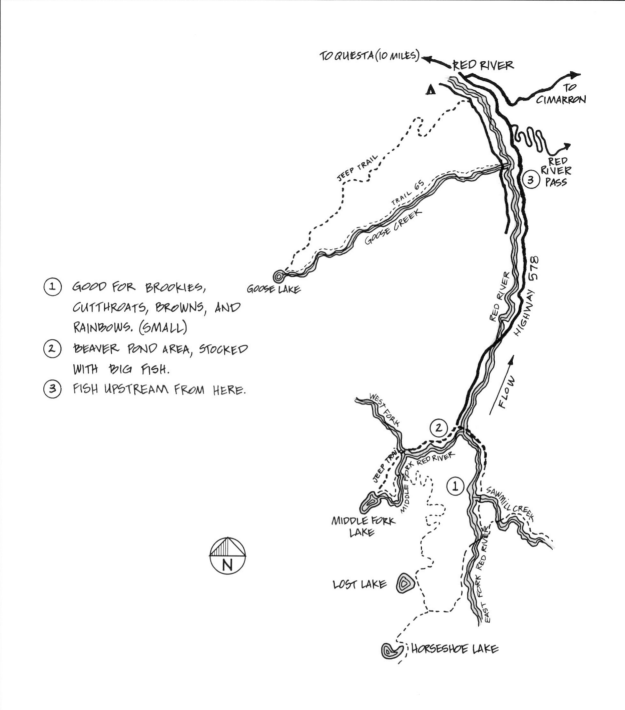

TO QUESTA (10 MILES)
RED RIVER
TO CIMARRON
JEEP TRAIL
TRAIL 65
GOOSE CREEK
RED RIVER PASS ③
GOOSE LAKE
RED RIVER
HIGHWAY 578
FLOW

① GOOD FOR BROOKIES, CUTTHROATS, BROWNS, AND RAINBOWS. (SMALL)

② BEAVER POND AREA, STOCKED WITH BIG FISH.

③ FISH UPSTREAM FROM HERE.

WEST FORK
②
JEEP TRAIL
MIDDLE FORK RED RIVER
①
SAWMILL CREEK
MIDDLE FORK LAKE

N

LOST LAKE
EAST FORK RED RIVER

HORSESHOE LAKE

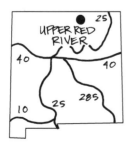

UPPER RED RIVER
25
40   40
10   25   285

UPPER RED RIVER

NOT TO SCALE

Red River

The Red River inspires people in different ways. The serious fly fisher envisions big trout tearing line from the reel while standing in the wild, lower river. Others despair the blue-gray water below the barren slopes of the mine. Some only think of the tourists near the town of Red River. Then there's the fine views everyone appreciates. This river offers all of this. Some history is important, however, before even a quick, No Nonsense vision of fly fishing the Red comes into focus.

Twenty years ago the lower Red was as good a natural trout stream as one could find. Four of us, including my brother Jackson, once caught 200, 1-4 lb. Cutbows in one day. Another day, after breaking my flyrod in half landing a 2 pounder, I caught three 19" cutbows with just the butt section of the rod. Allow, if you must, for exaggeration — that was great fishing. That was then.

In the 80's the effects of large-scale mining almost killed the river and its great fly fishing. Now, with the mine temporarily closed, the Red is recovering. There are plenty of fish with an occasional good one. As of this writing, the mine may re-open and the same problems may again befall the Red River. For now, however, this is a great fly fishing water on the mend, yet still enjoyable.

May - November the town of Red River stocks the upper waters with $35,000 worth of trout! None are under 14". Some weigh up to 20 pounds! When fish are planted right near town there's a spectacle more fun to view than join. A series of beaver ponds (several miles up the West Fork) is also stocked. A special regulation section, from Goose Creek upstream, is planned. It will also be stocked with lunkers.

Below town, the Red is mostly fishless from the mine to the hatchery. Rich spring water from the hatchery creates a year-round fishery of the four remaining, and rugged river miles.

Types of Fish
Browns, rainbow, some cutthroat and brook trout in upper river.

Known Hatches
Upper river: Caddis, midge, mayfly, spruce moth and terrestrials.
Lower river: Baetis (BWO), even on cold days.

Equipment to Use
Rods: 2-5 weight, 8 1/2 - 9'.
Reels: Palm or mechanical drag.
Line: Floating.
Leaders: 3x to 5x, 7 1/2'. 9' in beaver ponds.
Wading: Hippers in upper river, but water is cold. Chest waders best in lower river. Remove and wear wading shoes to hike out of canyon. Wet-wading often OK.

Flies to Use
Upper River
Dry Patterns: Royal Wulff, Humpy, attractors, #12-16.
Nymphs: Any small beadhead works OK.

Lower River
Dry Patterns: Blue-Winged Olive, well hackled for fast water #16-18.

Nymphs: Beadhead Hare's Ear #14-16, Peacock #10-14, Prince #12-16, Beadhead Caddis #12-14. Nymph deep, add lead (weight) when needed.

Ponds
Elk Hair Caddis or Mothy with Magic Midge Beadhead dropper tied 18-24" behind.

When to Fish
Upper river: After runoff, mid-June - October 15.
Lower river: Year-around, except during runoff.

Seasons & Limits
Year-around, 6 fish per day in Upper Red. Year-around, 4 fish per day in Lower Red. No tackle restrictions.

Accommodations & Services
Everything is available in Red River, including good fly shops. There's an outdoor store just east of Questa. Taos is close.

Nearby Fly Fishing
Columbine Creek for Rio Grande cutthroat (between Questa and Red River). Cabresto Creek has many small brookies and rainbows. Try Rio Grande and Cimarron Rivers, Middle Fork and Goose Lakes.

Rating
A 10 when you hook a large fish. Otherwise, a 7.5.

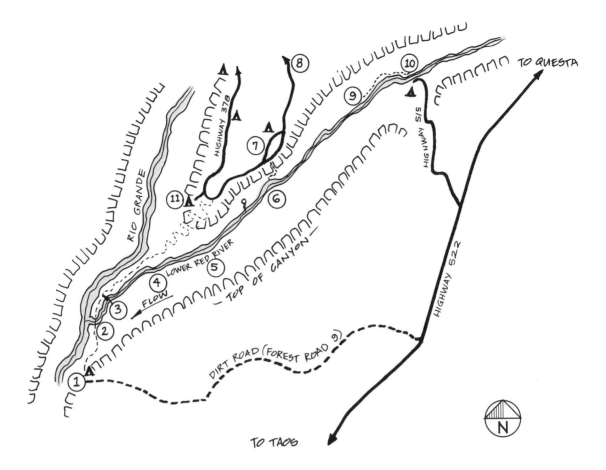

1. CEBOLLA MESA TRAIL TO LA JUNTA, 800 FEET DOWN.
2. LA JUNTA, FOOTBRIDGE OVER RED RIVER.
3. SHELTERS, TABLES, FIREPLACES.
4. GOOD WATER BETWEEN 2 AND 4. GETS ROUGH ABOVE.
5. FLAT AREA ON SOUTH BANK GOOD FOR CAMPING.
6. THREE SHELTERS WITH TABLES.
7. EL AGUAJE, CAMPING AND TRAIL. (500 FEET DOWN TO RIVER.)
8. RIO GRANDE WILD AND SCENIC RIVER VISITOR CENTER.
9. ROCK WALL. GOOD BETWEEN 6 AND 9. LOTS OF FISH.
10. FISH HATCHERY, PARKING, HIKING TRAIL TO 9. (45 MINUTE HIKE) OK FISHING BETWEEN 9 AND 10
11. LA JUNTA TRAILHEAD, PARKING & CAMPING

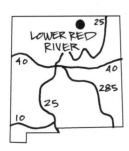

LOWER RED RIVER

NOT TO SCALE

Nick Streit (left) and father and author Taylor Streit hard at work in Northern New Mexico.

Photo: Garrett Vene Klasen

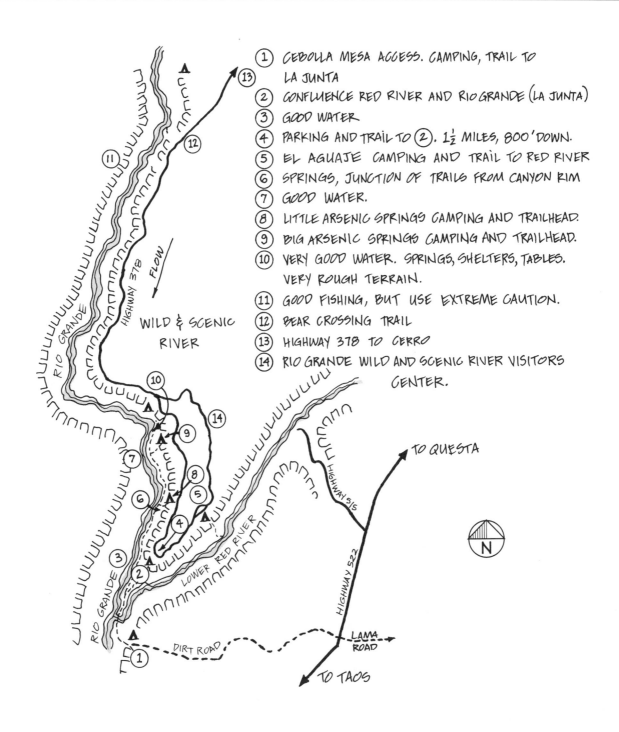

1. CEBOLLA MESA ACCESS. CAMPING, TRAIL TO LA JUNTA
2. CONFLUENCE RED RIVER AND RIO GRANDE (LA JUNTA)
3. GOOD WATER
4. PARKING AND TRAIL TO ②. 1½ MILES, 800' DOWN.
5. EL AGUAJE CAMPING AND TRAIL TO RED RIVER
6. SPRINGS, JUNCTION OF TRAILS FROM CANYON RIM
7. GOOD WATER.
8. LITTLE ARSENIC SPRINGS CAMPING AND TRAILHEAD.
9. BIG ARSENIC SPRINGS CAMPING AND TRAILHEAD.
10. VERY GOOD WATER. SPRINGS, SHELTERS, TABLES. VERY ROUGH TERRAIN.
11. GOOD FISHING, BUT USE EXTREME CAUTION.
12. BEAR CROSSING TRAIL
13. HIGHWAY 378 TO CERRO
14. RIO GRANDE WILD AND SCENIC RIVER VISITORS CENTER.

TO QUESTA

TO TAOS

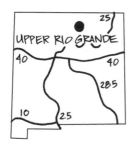

UPPER RIO GRANDE

NOT TO SCALE

Rio Grande
- Upper River -

This is fly fishing for the technically advanced, physically fit and adventurous. If this is not your profile, skim this section, then read Rio Grande -Lower River-.

My general division line for upper and lower Rio Grande is at the junction of the Red River and the Rio Grande. The upper canyon is topographically harsher. The lower has suffered from the influences of mining near the Red River. Though currently fishing well, renewed mining activity could repeat a sad story for trout and fly fishing in this area. Adventurous, hiking anglers are probably better off on the upper "Rio".

This upper section, tame at the Colorado border, slices about 800 feet into the earth by the time it reaches Arsenic Springs, about 20 miles south. Infusions from the rich springs have doubled the flow, making this a large and turbulent river.

Leave the wild upper 20 miles of river to the rattlers and eagles. Better access and fly fishing water starts at Bear Crossing. Here the river makes up for lost time by plunging over, under, around, and between huge basalt boulders. This is fantastic trout water, but dangerous going. Getting around is a 10 on the degree of difficulty scale --true "guerrilla" fly fishing. Especially when you must also make your way, on foot, over, under, around and between these big, slick rocks. Figure on a 30 minute hike in *and* a 45 minute hike back out. Some tips: Avoid cumbersome wading gear. Remove chest waders when hiking the canyon lest you drown in your own sweat. Pay attention to your every step on shore and in the river. Watch for drop-offs and deep water.

Being a good hand with a fly rod is important here, too. Confusing currents make it tough to make a good, deep, natural drift whit a nymph; in fact this is often impossible. One must then fish big Woolly Buggers, Muddlers and wet flies across the current. This is technical fishing. If you can afford a guide, this is the place to have one.

Just one day on this river section should give you plenty of stories. They may be more enjoyable to recall than experience. For example, our last trip produced a broken rod, reel and a slip that filled chest waders to the brim. Not many fish were caught and the long hike out ended in the dark with panting, sweating and swearing. The phrase "I'll never go back." was uttered.

Of course next October I'll suggest the voyage again, recalling only the huge brown my son almost landed. Plus there's that exciting feeling one gets entering this awesome and beautiful place. It makes one want to return. The "I'll never go back." declaration will be long forgotten.

Types of Fish
Cutbow, rainbow and brown trout, 12-20", some bigger.

Known Hatches
Caddis, Blue-Wing Olive, midge (winter), crayfish, minnows.

Equipment to Use
Rods: 5-7 weight, 8 - 9 1/2'.
Reels: Click drag.
Line: Floating. Sink tip in big deep pools OK.
Leaders: 2x to 4x, 9'. Or, all 3x tippet with shot to make nymph sink fast.
Wading: Rubber lug-soles for dry rocks or felt-soled boots. Wading wet is best unless cold.

Flies to Use
Dry Patterns: Usually fish nymphs, but try Elk Hair Caddis #14-16, attractors, hoppers near banks.

Nymphs & Streamers: Double Hackle Peacock #8-14, Poundmeister #8-10, Beadhead Hare's Ear #12-18, various beadheads #10-16, Brown or Gray Hackle #10-14, Black, Olive Woolly Bugger #4-10, Brown or Yellow Marabou Muddler, Platte River Specials #2-8.

When to Fish
Usually not until September. Best in October and the first half of November. If low and clear in spring or summer, fish after the sun leaves the water (5pm). Fish mid-day in the late fall.

Seasons & Limits
Year-around, 4 fish. Check New Mexico Game & Fish regulations to be sure.

Accommodations & Services
Sporting good store with licenses and flies just east of Questa. Fly shops in Taos and Red River. Questa has motels, cafes, gas, etc. Taos has everything and is 20 miles south.

Nearby Fly Fishing
Taos area, Costilla, Red, Lower Rio Grande rivers.

Rating
Hard work, awesome beauty, solitude, big fish and a great place to test your rod's warranty, a 9.

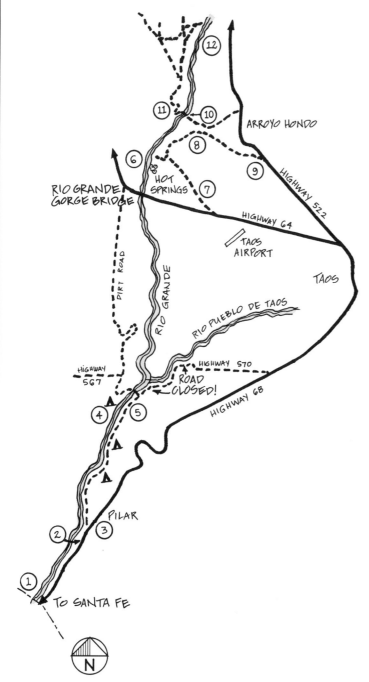

1. COUNTY LINE... GOOD WATER
2. PARKING, COVERED PICNIC TABLES. FISH UPRIVER PAST LONE PINE.
3. PHONE, CAFE, HOSTEL AT PILAR
4. OLD STATE PARK. EASY AND GOOD FISHING FROM ③ TO ⑤. FEE CAMPING AND DAY USE AREA, BRING A FEW BUCKS!
5. **TAOS JUNCTION BRIDGE**
6. MANBY HOT SPRINGS, STAGECOACH TRAIL. FISH UPRIVER, VERY GOOD WATER.
7. TURN RIGHT PAST AIRPORT, (DIRT ROAD, GOOD CONDITION) STAY ON GOOD ROAD HEADING DOWNHILL TOWARDS NORTHWEST.
8. TO MANBY HOT SPRINGS TURN SOUTH AS ROAD HEADS DOWNHILL. STAY ON (VERY ROUGH) ROAD... MAYBE 4×4 ONLY.
9. LEFT TURN FROM HIGHWAY BEFORE IT HEADS DOWNHILL. (FROM TAOS)
10. JOHN DUNN BRIDGE. GOOD FISHING DOWNRIVER
11. TURN RIGHT AT OLD GRAVEL PIT AT TOP OF CANYON, HEAD NORTH $1\frac{1}{2}$ MILES. RIGHT TURN AT "Y," STAY ON MOST USED ROAD UNTIL DEAD END AT TRAIL, $3\frac{1}{2}$ MILES FROM ⑪. ROUGH ROAD, 2WD TRUCK OK.
12. CEDAR SPRINGS... TRAIL 1 MILE LONG, VERY GOOD WATER UPRIVER OR DOWNRIVER

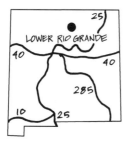

LOWER RIO GRANDE

NOT TO SCALE

Rio Grande

- Lower River -

The upper Rio Grande may be black-belt fly fishing. The lower river has water for every skill level. Despite being along the highway, the lower stretch, from the Taos county line up-river, is fished lightly. If it looks too rough for you, very easy access and wading is available just above Pilar. The river is heavily stocked year around.

Above the Taos Junction bridge the river's character changes drastically as it enters the "Taos Box". The river is wilder here and only a few rugged trails get you into an area that is virtually unfished.

From the John Dunn Bridge down river the river is rafted extensively from spring to early summer. This is probably not a great bother to the fish but is to many anglers. Rafting trips leave John Dunn Bridge in AM, travel through "the box" and reach Taos Junction bridge in PM. Rafters are also common below Pilar, generally from 9 AM to 5 PM. If you wish to avoid conflicts plan fishing trips accordingly. Fortunately, most of the Rio fishes best at either end of the day this time of year.

The gorge and river become tamer above Manby Hot Springs. The only vehicular access for the area is at the John Dunn bridge. Upstream, dead-drift, nymph fishing is your best bet here and on most of the rest of the Rio Grande as well.

Above the John Dunn bridge there are several miles of river with grassy banks and relatively easy going. Foot trails are the only means of access, the best choice being those near Cedar Springs.

Timing is critical on these stretches, as the lower Rio seldom fishes well until September. It's usually even better in late October if the normally excellent Blue-Winged Olive hatch occurs. This hatch gives way to winter dry fly fishing when "Snow flies" (midges) hatch late in the day. Drive along the river and look for risers. In April, just before run-off, a blizzard caddis fly hatch may occur, but this hatch and the river conditions can be iffy.

Remember that the elevation at the bottom of the gorge is well over 6000'. Hiking up several hundred feet to the canyon rim will have you panting hard.

Types of Fish
Rainbow, cutbow and brown trout averaging 10-15".

Known Hatches
Caddis (varied and numerous), cranefly, Blue-Wing Olive (fall) snowfly, midges and hoppers.

Equipment to Use
Rods: 4 - 6 weight, 8 1/2 - 9'.
Reels: Palm or mechanical drag.
Line: Floating.
Leaders: 3x to 5x, 9'.
Wading: Chest high neoprene waders. In hot weather, wet-wade.

Flies to Use
Dry Patterns: Tan Elk Hair and Solomon Caddis #14-18, Blue Winged Olive #16-20, Snowfly #18-22, Snowfly Cluster #16-18, Griffith's Gnat #18-20, Hoppers, Plopper #8-12, attractors #12-16.

Wet Patterns: Double Hackle Peacock #8-14, Beadhead Hare's Ear #12-16, Beadhead Caddis #14, Poundmeister #8-10, Black Woolly Bugger, Muddler #4-10.

When to Fish
September to mid-November is prime. Winter snowfly fishing lasts until March. It's good in the spring and summer if the water isn't high and muddy. Fall fishing is best mid-day. Winter fishing is best in the late afternoon.

Seasons & Limits
Year around, 4-fish limit in "The Box".

Accommodations & Services
Taos, para todo.
Translation: for everything, go to Taos.

Nearby Fly Fishing
See the Taos Area section. In winter, try the Chama below Abiquiu.

Rating
Over the years the rating goes up or down with the price of molybdenum, but generally an 8.

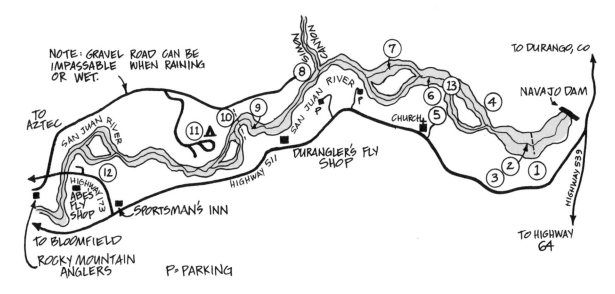

NOTE: GRAVEL ROAD CAN BE IMPASSABLE WHEN RAINING OR WET.

P= PARKING

① FEE PARKING, BRING SEVERAL DOLLAR BILLS
② CABLE. CATCH AND RELEASE ABOVE
③ FEE PARKING, TRAIL TO UPPER FLATS
④ UPPER FLATS, GOOD FOR DRY FLIES (MIDGES)
⑤ TEXAS HOLE PARKING (FEE) CROWDED WITH FISH AND FISHERMEN.
⑥ BAETIS BEND
⑦ LOWER FLATS
⑧ SIMON CANYON: FEWER FISH, BUT GOOD MAYFLY HATCHES
⑨ FEWER BUT BIGGER FISH POSSIBLE
⑩ BOUNDARY SPECIAL REGULATION WATER, BUT STILL GOOD FISHING FOR SMALLER TROUT BELOW... SOME LARGE BROWNS
⑪ COTTONWOOD CAMPGROUND
⑫ SPORTSMAN'S INN (GOOD BURGERS!) AND RIZUTO'S FLY SHOP
⑬ TEXAS HOLE

NOTE: SEVERAL PAY STATIONS ALONG RIVER

SAN JUAN RIVER

NOT TO SCALE

San Juan River

Very cold (42°) water flows from the dam at huge Navajo Lake. This creates an oasis for wildlife, rainbow trout and fly fishers in what is an otherwise parched sandstone landscape. This is also home to tiny flies, light tippets and big fish that can provide thrilling fly fishing in short order. This is New Mexico's premiere fly fishing destination. The rest is legendary.

There are many big trout here. There are also *lots* of anglers. This can strain tempera-ments, so fly fishing etiquette is ever important. Give others as much room as possible, stay on the trails, and please don't wade through feeding fish. You can avoid the crowds (some-what) by staying away from parking areas, exploring side channels and trying off peak winter and high flow periods when fishing is can be quite good.

This said, fly fishing the challenging San Juan is often mystifying. Even very skilled anglers may bat zero while the guy one rock away hauls them in; while using the same fly no less. You'll also see big trout feed on what seems to be nothing. Use your entire bag of fly fishing tricks on this river. If you've not fished here before, *hire a qualified guide*. This helps to de-mystify things and gets beginners into big fish. *(Editors note: Beginners* probably won't *catch fish here without a guide. They'll catch many fish here* with *Taylor Streit.)*

Most fish are caught using nymphs drifted along the bottom. Excellent sight fishing, using dry flies is also possible. Nothing beats seeing the perfect drift meet with the white jaws of a visible fish.

As mentioned, the water is very cold. Much of the wading here is easy, but use extra caution in the main channel. Neoprene chest-high waders with felt-soled boots are required. Local shops and guides rent them. In summer, your top half fries. Wear a hat, long sleeves and sun block. In winter, dress *very* warmly.

Types of Fish
Rainbows and browns (more browns down river).

Known Hatches
Usually hatches occur midday. Fish prefer nymph to the adult. Dry fly fishing best on still days.
Midges: Year around.
PMD's: Summer and early fall.
Baetis: Spring and fall.
Caddis: Summer (down river).
Hoppers: Summer and fall.

Equipment to Use
Rods: 4 - 6 weight, 8 1/2 - 9'. Stiff rods can break the light tippets used here.
Reels: Mechanical drag best for big fish.
Line: Floating.
Leaders: 5x to 7x, 9'. Hooks #16-28 use 4x to 5x, 9'.
Wading: Neoprene chest-high waders and boots.

Flies to Use
Dry Patterns: Magic Midge (wet or dry) #18-22 Midge #20-28, Griffith's Gnat #16-24, Black or Gray CDC Midge Adult #20-28, Comparadun, Sparkle Dun, CDC Transitional Dun, Blue Winged Olive #18-24, Parachute Adams #16-24, Brown or Olive Elk Hair Caddis (June-July), Comparadun PMD (July-Sept.), Sparkle Dun PMD (July-Sept.), CDC Tran. Dun PMD (July-Sept.) #16-18, Hopper (July-September) #8-12.

Nymphs: Black, Brown, or Olive Midge Pupa #20-28, Cream & Olive Midge Larva, Copper or Red Brassie, Disco Midge, Brown & Gray WD 40 #18-24, Pheasant Tail #16-20, Red, Orange & Pink Analids #16-22.

Use these all year (best Winter & Spring): Red, Orange or Tan San Juan Worm #12-14, Black, Brown or Olive Woolly Bugger #6-10, Black, Brown or Olive Rabbit Leech #6-10, PMD nymph #16 (July-September).

When to Fish
Year around, but summer - fall is best (also the most crowded).

Seasons & Limits
Catch and release above the cable. Cable down river 3 1/2 miles, 1 fish over 20". Below that, 6 fish per day.

Nearby Fly Fishing
Nothing close, but the Durango area has lots of fishing.

Accommodations & Services
Lodging, groceries, gas, licenses at the river or in Aztec (a nice town). Twenty miles west is Farmington, a city with an airport and numerous facilities. Note: Make reservations well in advance for lodging and guides. For parking on the river, bring 3 $1 bills.

Rating
This is New Mexico's best-known fly fishing river, a 9.

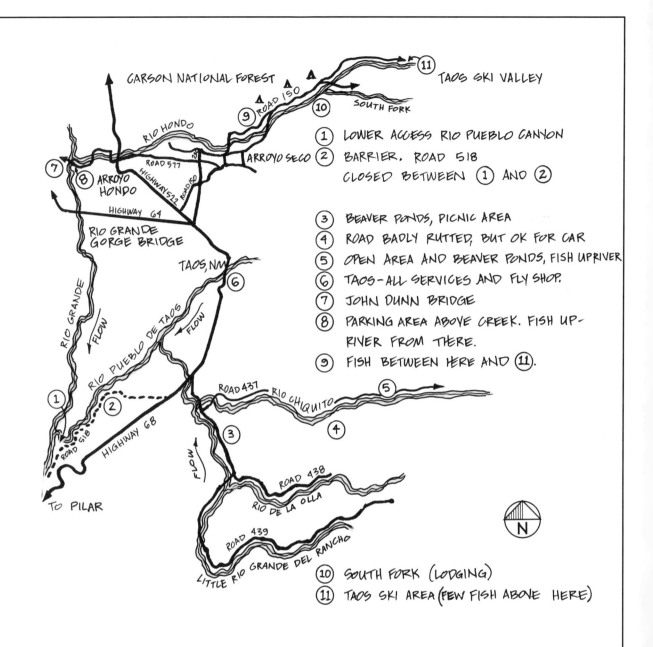

CARSON NATIONAL FOREST

TAOS SKI VALLEY

RIO HONDO

ROAD 150

SOUTH FORK

⑨ ⑩

ARROYO SECO

ROAD 577

⑦

⑧ ARROYO HONDO

HIGHWAY 512

ROAD 150

HIGHWAY 64

RIO GRANDE GORGE BRIDGE

TAOS, NM

⑥

RIO GRANDE

FLOW

RIO PUEBLO DE TAOS

FLOW

ROAD 437   RIO CHIQUITO   ⑤

① ②

ROAD 518

HIGHWAY 68

③

④

FLOW

ROAD 438

RIO DE LA OLLA

ROAD 439

LITTLE RIO GRANDE DEL RANCHO

TO PILAR

N

① LOWER ACCESS RIO PUEBLO CANYON
② BARRIER. ROAD 518
   CLOSED BETWEEN ① AND ②

③ BEAVER PONDS, PICNIC AREA
④ ROAD BADLY RUTTED, BUT OK FOR CAR
⑤ OPEN AREA AND BEAVER PONDS, FISH UPRIVER
⑥ TAOS-ALL SERVICES AND FLY SHOP.
⑦ JOHN DUNN BRIDGE
⑧ PARKING AREA ABOVE CREEK. FISH UP-
   RIVER FROM THERE.
⑨ FISH BETWEEN HERE AND ⑪.

⑩ SOUTH FORK (LODGING)
⑪ TAOS SKI AREA (FEW FISH ABOVE HERE)

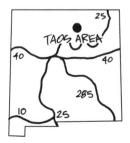

25

TAOS AREA

40   40

285

10   25

TAOS AREA

NOT TO SCALE

Taos Area

Taos is an excellent headquarters for fly fishers visiting New Mexico. One can fly fish all day, return to sophisticated digs in town, have a great meal and hear happy tales from non-fishing family members. Their day in the unique town and beautiful valley will have been eventful as well. Fly fish and relax in Taos — the credit card bill won't arrive for a month.

A third of the waters in this guide are within a 90 minute drive from Taos. Fish them week days, if you can manage. Certainly avoid the lower Hondo and Rio Chiquito on weekends.

The Rio Hondo, with two distinct stretches, is only 10 miles north of Taos. There's drive-by fishing on the lower river, just before it enters the Rio Grande. Park before the road climbs out of the canyon and fish upstream. The upper Hondo is a fast, clear and cold little river. Often brushy, it's full of wild cutbows, browns and hatchery trout.

There's about 50 miles of 5 - 10' wide streams in the Little Rio Grande watershed. If you're looking for easy access to solitude, try the Rio Chiquito (Little River). Believe me, you'll need all the available solitude. It will absorb the cursing that comes from the twin sport of trying to catch spooky little trout and fighting attacking brush. Happily, some open areas and beaver ponds keep anglers quiet.

The Rio Pueblo De Taos is a medium sized creek that pours through a rugged canyon. Downstream from Taos, it unfortunately suffers from the town's sewage, trash and thirst for water. In spite of all this there are many good pools holding browns up to 20". There is a lot of trout food. The well-fed brown trout have little competition and feed sporadically. Anglers who hit this at the right time will land some beautiful fish.

Types of Fish
Brown and rainbow trout and cutbows.

Known Hatches
Hondo & Chiquito: Various mayflies and caddis.
Rio Pueblo de Taos: Cranefly larvae, minnows, ginger dun (summer evenings).

Equipment to Use
Rods: 2-5 weight, 7 - 9'.
Reels: Palm or mechanical drag.
Line: Floating.
Leaders: 3x to 5x, 7 1/2'.
Wading: Wet-wade in summer, hippers or chest-high neoprenes OK. Upper Hondo is cold & slippery, wear hippers.

Flies to Use
Lower Hondo
Dry Patterns: Elk Hair Caddis, various attractors, #14-16, Parachute Adams #14-18.
Nymphs: Peacock #12-14, Hare's Ear, Pheasant Tail #14-18, various beadheads #14-16.

Upper Hondo
Dry Patterns: Renegade, Humpy, various attractors #12-14. Nymphs unnecessary.

Rio Chiquito (Little Rio Grande) Watershed
Dry Patterns: Elk Hair Caddis, Mothy, various attractors #14-16. Nymphs unnecessary.

Rio Pueblo de Taos
Dry Patterns: Various attractors, Ginger Dun #14, Grasshoppers #8-10.

Nymphs & Streamers: Poundmeister #8-10, Double Hackle Peacock #10-14, various beadheads #12-14, Muddlers, Zonkers, Black Woolly Bugger #6-10.

When to Fish
Upper Hondo: Mid-day during mid-summer.
Lower Hondo: After runoff & late on summer evenings.
Rio Pueblo de Taos: End of runoff, late summer evenings, fall-early spring and mid-days in winter.
Rio Chiquito: Late-May through October.

Seasons & Limits
Fish year-around, no special regulations.

Accommodations & Services
Fly shop and all services in Taos.

Nearby Fly Fishing
Rio Grande, Cimarron, Costilla Rivers.

Rating
Something for everyone in Taos, a 7.

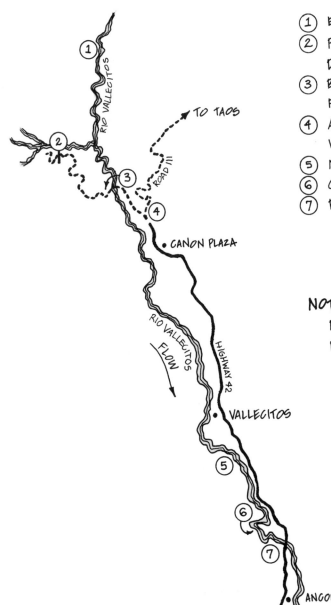

1. EL VALLECITOS RANCH (PRIVATE)
2. PARK SHORT OF GATE AND WALK DOWN CREEK TO RIVER.
3. BRIDGE. PARKING, PRIMITIVE CAMPING FISH UPSTREAM FROM BRIDGE.
4. ACCESS FROM TAOS VIA 111 (42) VERY LONG DRIVE!
5. NATIONAL FOREST BOUNDARY.
6. GOOD WATER AWAY FROM ROAD.
7. BRIDGE

NOTE: BETWEEN ③ AND ⑤ MOSTLY PRIVATE PROPERTY. ASK FOR PERMISSION TO FISH.

RIO VALLECITOS

NOT TO SCALE

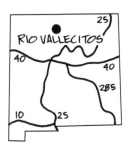

Rio Vallecitos

Like most of Northern New Mexico, the area near this water was settled by the Spanish centuries ago. Though, as the crow flies, not far from the sophisticated streets of Santa Fe, this area is worlds apart in other respects. Patients and good manners are valued here. Boundaries between public and private property may be unclear. Forest Service maps are excellent references. If you're in doubt, respectfully ask permission to fish.

The Vallecitos originates in the middle of New Mexico's San Juan Mountains. It flows almost entirely through private land until just below Vallecitos Ranch, where it enters the Carson National Forest. This is the fishable section.

A waterfall in this area creates a natural barrier for the smallish wild rainbows above and the browns and 'bows below. Reaching this section is considerable work so the water is seldom fished.

The 20' wide river enters "civilization" above the town of Cañon Plaza. The river tumbles lazily through several small valleys and their tiny towns. Access is limited on the few public lands bordering the river. The lower canyon (#6) is a good choice and has some decent fish. This is dry fly territory except for the deep pools where nymphs work best.

In normal summer weather the upper water fishes best from 11 AM to 3 PM. The warmer, downstream water fishes best somewhat earlier in the day. Excellent mayfly and caddis hatches are common on still, summer (especially humid) evenings. Low flow in the summer and fall make fly fishing more difficult. The stealthy angler will do well to avoid slow water, stay low and fish from the shade when possible.

Types of Fish
Rainbow and brown trout.

Known Hatches
Midges, caddis, spruce moth, various mayflies and Golden Stones found mostly in the upper river.

Equipment to Use
Rods: 2-5 weight, 8 - 9'.
Reels: Palm or mechanical drag.
Line: Floating.
Leaders: 3x to 4x, 7 1/2 - 9'.
Wading: Very slick rocks in upper water. Dunkings are common. Hippers are OK, but chest-high waders keep one dry. Use felt-soled boots. Wet-wade in summer.

Flies to Use
Dry Patterns: Attractors like Wulffs, Colorado King, Humpy, etc., #14-16. Mothy #10-12, Parachute Adams, Elk Hair Caddis #12-16, Terminator #12.

Nymphs: Various beadheads #12-16, Zug Bug, Hare's Ear #14-16, Peacock #12-14.

When to Fish
When runoff drops, around June 1, until early October.

Seasons & Limits
Year around, six fish per day.

Accommodations & Services
Lodging and cafes are south in Ojo Caliente (Hot Spring). Bath and sweat wrap, highly recommended. Store in La Madera. Primitive camping near bridge (#3 on map).

Rating
Tranquil area, relatively light fishing pressure and many fish combine for a 7.5.

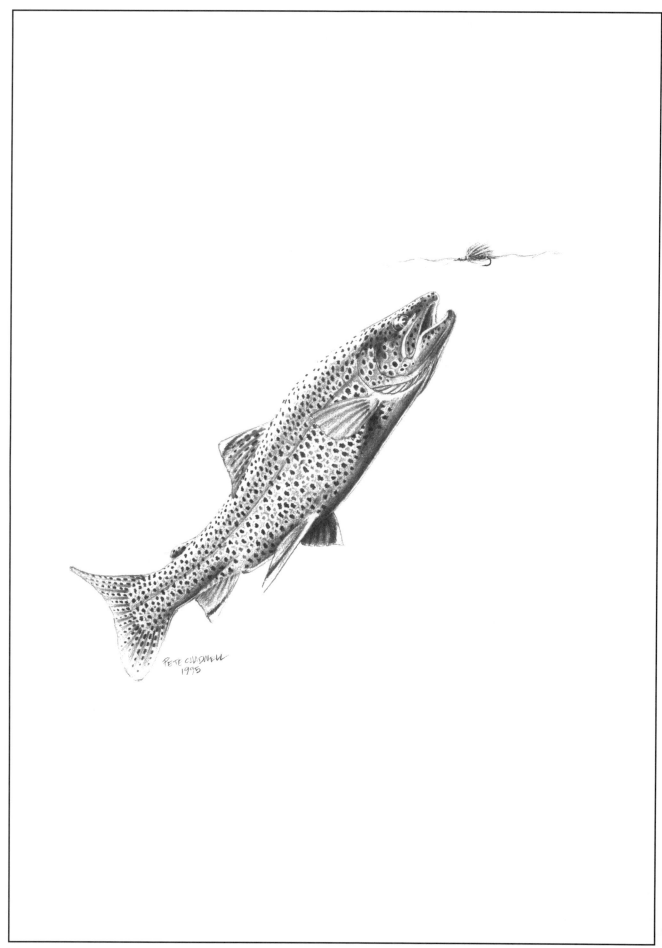

Appendix

New Mexico Fly Tackle

North West

Fox Creek Store
2657 Highway 17
Antonito, CO 81120
(719) 376-5881

Duranglers
801 B. Main Avenue
Durango, CO 81301
(970) 385-4081

Dark Timber
Sporting Goods
2242 Main Street
Chama, NM 87520
(505) 756-2300

Rizuto's Fly Shop
P.O. Box 6309
1796 Highway 173
Navajo Dam, NM 87419
(505) 632-3893

Abe's Motel & Fly Shop
P.O. Box 6428
Highway 173
Navajo Dam, NM 87419
(505) 632-2194

Duranglers
On The San Juan
1003 Highway 511
Navajo Dam, NM 87419
(505) 632-5952

New Sportsman Inn
P.O. Box 6325
Navajo Dam, NM 87419
(505) 632-3271

Rocky Mountain Anglers
P.O. Box 6306
Navajo Dam, NM 87419
(505) 632-0445

North Central

Starr Angler Fly Shop
P.O. Box 729
300 East Main Street
Red River, NM 87558
(505) 754-2320

Williams Trading Post
P.O. Box 297
306 High Street
Red River, NM 87558
(505) 754-2217

Taylor Streit
Fly Fishing Service
P.O. Box 2759
Taos, New Mexico 87571
(505) 751-1312
www.streitflyfishing.com

Los Rios Anglers
P.O. Box 4006
226 'C' N. Pueblo Rd.
Taos, New Mexico 87571
(505) 758-2798

Central

Oshman's
1404 Cerillos Road
(Villa Linda Mall)
Santa Fe, NM 82502
(505) 473-3555

Reel Life
510 Montezuma Street
Santa Fe, NM 87501
(505) 995-8114

High Desert Angler
435 S. Guadalupe
Santa Fe, NM 87501
(505) 98TROUT

Timberline Sports
1408 A Chama Highway
Espanola, NM 87532
(505) 753-8747

Albuquerque Area

Los Pinos Fly Shop
2820 Richmond Drive N.E.
Albuquerque, NM 87107
(800) 594-9637
(505) 884-7501

Reel Life
1100 San Mateo Suite #60
Albuquerque, NM 87110
(505) 268-1693

Charlie's Sporting Goods
8908 Menaul NE
Albuquerque, NM 87112
(505) 275-3006

Gardenswartz Sports
2720 San Mateo NE
Albuquerque, NM 87110

Oshman's
2100 Louisiana Blvd. N.E.
(Winrock Mall)
Albuquerque, NM 87110
(505) 881-8082

Dos Amigos Trading Co.
US Highway 64
P.O. Drawer 377
Eagle Nest, NM 87718
(505) 377-6226

South

The Anglers Nook
2711 Claude Dove Drive
Las Cruces, NM 88011
(505) 522-3810

Fly's Etc.
Timbers Mall
2553 Sudderth
Ruidoso, NM 88345
(505) 257-4968

Carrillo's Fly Shop
P.O. Box 194
Central, NM 88026
(505) 537-3793

Clubs & Associations

New Mexico Trout
P.O. Box 8553 Station C
Albuquerque, NM 87198
(505)344-6363

Amigos Bravos
P.O. Box 238
Taos, NM 87571
(505) 758-3874

Federation of Fly Fishers
National Headquarters
1(800) 618-0808
Call for local club

International Game
Fish Association
300 Gulf Stream Way
Dana Beach, FL 33004
(954) 927-2628

National Fresh Water
Fishing Hall of Fame
P.O. Box 33
Hayward, WI 54843
(715) 634-4440

Guidebooks

www.amazon.com

www.bookzone.com

www.powells.com

www.booksnow.com

www.justgoodbooks.com

www.adventuroustraveler.com

www.barnesandnoble.com

Fly Fishing The Internet

www.worldflyfish.com

www.flyshop.com

www.fbn-flyfish.com

www2.flyfishamerica.com

www. gofishing.com

www.ffa.com

www.fly-fishing-women.com

www.tu.org/troutor

www.flyfishing.com.asf

www.ool.com/fff

www.ohwy.com

www.amrivers.org

www.gorp.com

www.flyfishto.com

www.flyfish.com

Directories

www.onbasetech.com/marc/fish.html

www.flyfishing.miningco.com

www.zoomnet.net/~tron/ifr.html

www.fish-world.com

Knots

www.earlham.edu/~peters/knotlink.html

www.ozemail.com.au/~fnq/fishing

Additional Information

Fishing Resources

1(800) ASK FISH
For general New Mexico fishing and camping information.

Albuquerque Journal
Weekly column in this newspaper covers fishing and current conditions. (usually printed on Thursday).

New Mexico Great Outdoors
Monthly magazine.
(505) 2982190

Water Flow Rates
Abiquiu Dam
1 (800) 843-3029
El Vado Dam
(505) 756-7175

U.S.G.S.
Public Water
Resource Division
(505) 262-5300
(Ask for information officer)

Maps
Branch of Distribution
U.S.G.S.
Box 25286
Denver, CO 80225
(303) 202-4700

Recreation & Facilities

New Mexico Dept.
Of Tourism
P.O. Box 20003
Santa Fe, NM 87503
(505) 827-0291
1 (800) 545-2040
(NM Vacation Guide)

Indian Country
Tourism Council
P.O. Box 1
Church Rock, NM 87311
1(800) 233-4528

Government Resources

New Mexico Department
of Game & Fish
(5 offices)
P.O. Box 25112
Santa Fe, NM 87504
(505) 827-7911
Fisheries Division
(505) 827-7905

Albuquerque
3841 Midway Place NW
Albuquerque, NM 87109
(505) 841-8881

Las Cruces
566 North Telshor Blvd.
Las Cruces, NM 88011
(505) 522-9796

Roswell
1912 West Second St.
Roswell, NM 88201
(505) 624-6135

Raton
153 Bacon St.
Raton, NM 87740
(505) 445-2311

U.S. Fish
& Wildlife Service
P.O. Box 1306
Albuquerque, NM 87103
(505) 766-3940

BLM
1475 Rodeo Rd.
Santa Fe, NM 87505
(505) 438-7400

BLM
224 Cruz Alta Rd.
Taos, NM 87571
(505) 758-8851

National Park Service
P.O. Box 728
Santa Fe, NM 87504
(505) 988-6012

Bureau of Indian Affairs
615 First St. NW
Albuquerque, NM 87102

Forest Service Offices

Carson National Forest
Forest Service Bldg.
208 Cruz Alta Road
Taos, NM 87571
(505) 758-6200

Cibola National Forest
2113 Osuna Rd. NE,
Suite A
Albuquerque, NM 87113
(505) 761-4650

Gila National Forest
3005 E. Camino Bosque
Silver City, NM 88061
(505) 388-8201

Lincoln National Forest
1101 New York
Alamogordo, NM 88310
(505) 434-7200

Santa Fe National. Forest
1220 St. Francis Drive
P.O. Box 1689
Santa Fe, NM 87504
(505) 988-6940

State Parks, Forestry & Campgrounds

State Parks & Recreation
408 Galisteo
Santa Fe, NM 87504
888-667-2757

Dept. of Forestry
P.O. Box 458
Bernalillo, NM 87004
(505) 867-2334

National Forest &
National Park
Campgrounds
1(800) 280-2267

Maps

Gila Hike & Bike
Silver City, NM
(505) 388-3222

Brodsky Book Shop
Taos, NM
(505) 758-9468

Holman's Inc.
Albuquerque, NM
(505) 343-0007

BLM & Intermediate
Scale Maps
P.O. Box 1449
Santa Fe, 87540
(505) 988-6000

City, County, Hwy Maps
NM Highway &
Transportation Dept.
1120 Cerrillos Rd.
Santa Fe, NM 87501
(505) 827-5250

References & Other Reading

Fly Fishing Southern New Mexico
Rex Johnson
Ron Smorynski
University Of NM Press

The Lakes of New Mexico
Andy Sandersien
University Of NM Press

Fly Fishing Northern New Mexico
Craig Martin
University Of NM Press

Fishing In New Mexico
Ty Piper
University Of NM Press

The Roads of New Mexico (Atlas)
Shearer Publishing

South West Camping
Fog Horn Press

No Nonsense Fly Fishing Knots

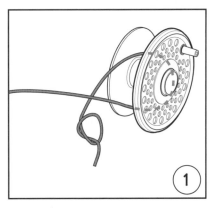
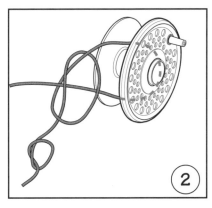
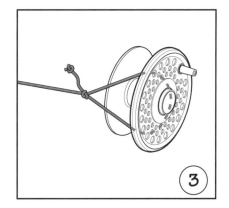

Arbor Knot Use this knot to attach backing to your fly reel. 75 yards of backing will be plenty for most waters.

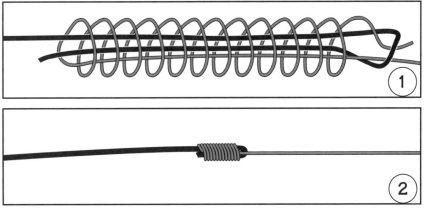

Albright Knot Use this knot to connect backing to the fly line or shooting line

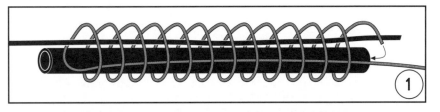

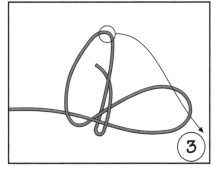

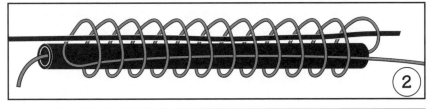

FLY LINE

LEADER

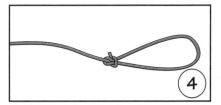

Nail Knot Use a nail, needle or a small tube to tie this knot, which connects the forward end of the fly line to the butt end of the leader. Follow this with a Perfection Loop, and you've got a permanent end loop that allows easy leader changes.

Perfection Loop Use this knot to create a loop in the butt end of the leader. You can easily "loop-to-loop" your leader to your fly line.

No Nonsense Fly Fishing Knots

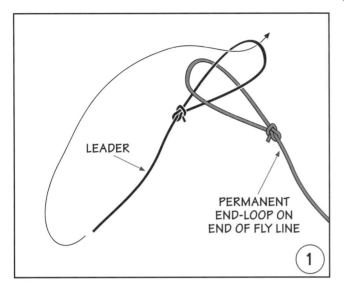

Loop To Loop Use this simple knot to connect the leader to an end loop on the tip of the fly line

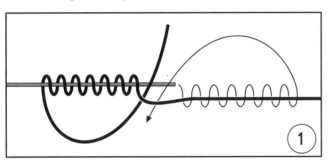

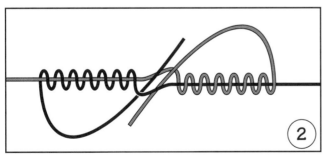

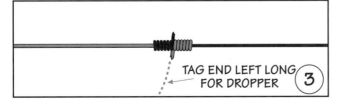

Blood Knot Use this knot to connect sections of leader material. To add a dropper, leave the heavier tag end long and attach fly.

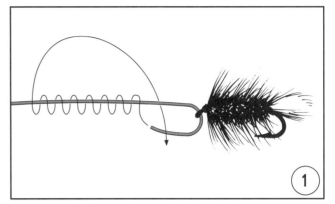

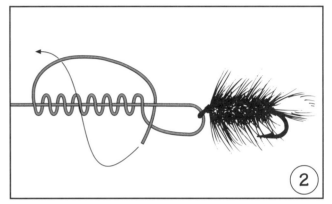

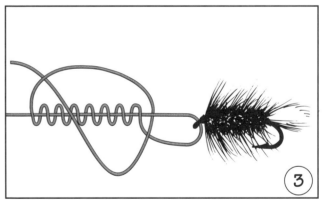

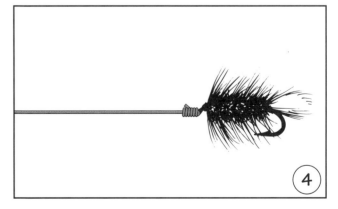

Improved Clinch Knot Use this knot to attach a fly to the end of the tippet. Remember to moisten the knot just before you pull it tight.

Fly Fishing Terms
Especially for the Beginner

Action adj. Used to describe the relative resistance to bending as you move down the length of a particular fly rod.

Attractor n. A fly that is designed to look like no life form in particular, but rather to just attract the attention of the quarry and give the impression of being something good to eat.

Backing n. A very strong, thin braided line tied to the fly reel and to which you attach the fly line itself.

Barbless adj. A type of hook which does not have a barb on the pointed end. Barbs were thought to assist in keeping the hook from being shaken lose by the fish. Research shows barbless hooks hold as well if tension is kept on the line by the fisher.

Beadhead adj. Describes a nymph or wetfly which has a small brass or chrome bead placed on the hook ahead of the fly pattern.

Blood Knot n. A knot used to tie tippet material to the end of a leader. A very difficult knot to tie.

Bluegill n. A small, warm-water sunfish found just about everywhere in America.

Brook Trout n. (Salvelinus fontinalis) A trout-like fish indigenous to the Northeast and Midwest United States. Not actually a trout but rather a member of the Char family.

Brown Trout n. (Salmo trutta) A trout originally indigenous to Europe, Brown Trout can now be found all over America and Canada, as well as many other countries in the world.

Caddis Fly n. (Order Trichoptera) A very common waterborne insect with wings held back and up at a 45 degree angle.

Catch and Release n. The practice of releasing all fish caught with a fly rod unharmed. It is based on a value that the fishing experience is more important than keeping fish.

Char n. (Salvelinus) American Brook Trout and Lake Trout are examples of Char found in the United States. Char are cousins of trout, and breed with them, but their offspring are sterile.

Cranefly n. The "Daddy Longlegs" of the flying insect world, they are fished mainly as terrestrials, and can be fished very effectively in late summer and early fall.

Cutthroat Trout n. (Oncorhynchus clarki) A trout originally indigenous to the Western drainages of the Rocky Mountains, it is distinguished by red throat slashes under its jaw.

Damselfly n. (Enallagma cyathigarum) A large aquatic fly characterized by a long skinny, blue thorax and wings that are held back at an angle.

Disk Drag n. A mechanical method of applying resistance to fly line as it is drawn out by a fish that is hooked.

Dolly Varden n. A Char that often runs to the sea.

Dun n. The stage of a waterborne insect just after it has emerged and has the ability to fly.

Emerger n. That stage in the development of a waterborne insect when it leaves its shuck and emerging into a flying insect.

False Cast v. The act of forecasting and backcasting without ever delivering the fly to the water.

Ferrule n. The method used to join two sections of a fly rod.

Fly Fishing n. The highest form of fishing.

Fly Line n. The thick-bodied line attached to the backing, which is used to actually cast the fly.

Fry n. A baby fish.

Grayling n. (Thymallus thymallus) An elegant looking member of the salmonid family of fish that looks like a silver colored trout (but isn't a trout) and has a very large dorsal (top) fin.

Hatch n. The time when a species of waterborne insect is emerging and becoming a flying insect.

Improved Clinch Knot n. A knot used to tie a fly to the end of a leader or to a tippet.

Keeper n. A small wire ring located just in front of the grip or handle on a fly rod.

Lake Trout n. (Salvelinus namaycush) Not real trout, they are members of the Char family. They not only live in lakes, they also spawn there.

Leader n. A thin, clear monofilament tapered line attached to the end of the fly line, to which either the tippet or fly is attached.

Loading n. The act of bending a fly rod at the end of a back cast, which is caused by the weight of the fly line transferring its weight into stored energy held in the bent fly rod.

Mayfly n. (Order Ephemeroptera) A very common waterborne insect characterized by wings held in a nearly vertical position.

Mend v. To move the fly line upstream from the fly.

Midge n. (Order Diptera) A very small, mosquito-type fly often imitated by fly tiers.

Nail Knot n. A common knot used to tie the backing to the fly line and the leader to the fly line.

Nipper n. a device used to cut line quickly and neatly.

Nymph n. An undeveloped insect. Nymphs live under the water for months prior to emerging into a winged insect.

Pack Rod n. A fly rod that breaks down into between 3 and 6 pieces, which allows it to be packed into remote areas easily.

Pool n. A location in a stream where the water is deeper than most other locations and the water runs slower.

Popper n. A floating lure used to catch warm-water fish such as bass or bluegill.

More Fly Fishing Terms

Rainbow Trout n. (Oncorhynchus mykiss) A Trout which is indigenous to the Pacific drainages of the Rocky Mountains; it is known for the rich pinkish colorations along the center line of the fish.

Reach Cast n. A Cast which is used when fishing downstream or when your need extra slack in your line.

Rest the Water v. Allowing the water to calm down after some form of disturbance.

Rise v. A fish coming to the surface and feeding on some food source found there.

Roll Cast n. A cast used where there is little or no room behind the fisher for a backcast.

Run n. A location in a stream characterized by shallow running water over a rocky streambed that feeds into a pool.

Salmon n. A large member of the salmonidae fish family which hatch in fresh water and migrate to a lake or the ocean. Some return to the stream of their origin to spawn and then die.

Scud n. A very small cold water crustacean often erroneously referred to as "freshwater shrimp."

Sea Run adj. A term applied to trout that hatch in fresh water and then migrate to the sea to grow to adulthood, then return to their natal waters to spawn.

Shooting Line n. The act of releasing extra line held in the free hand as the line passes the caster in the forecast.

Shooting Taper adj. Used to describe a rather short (45-46 feet) fly line with a majority of the weight out at the front end.

Single Action adj. A fly reel that has fixed drag, set at the factory, that cannot be adjusted by the user.

Sink Tip adj. A floating fly line with about ten feet of sinking line built into, or attached to, the front end.

Spinner n. The final stage of a waterborne insect during the mating session, when it falls, fatigued, to the water and dies.

Spinner Fall n. That time when many thousands of waterborne insects like Mayflies and Caddis Flies fall to the water in their last mortal stage.

Spring Creek n. A stream that originates from water coming up from the ground, as opposed to a freestone stream which originates from run-off or snow melt.

Steelhead n. A type of Rainbow Trout that migrates from the stream or river in which it is hatched to the ocean or a large landlocked lake.

Stocker adj. Term used to describe a fish which was born and raised in a hatchery and then placed in a stream, river or lake for sport fishing purposes.

Stonefly n. (Order Plecoptera) A large aquatic fly that emerges by crawling out of the water onto a stone or rock and then splits its shuck and becomes a flying insect.

Streamer n. A fly that imitates a small fish, worm, leech, etc.

Strike Indicator n. A floating substance, most commonly foam or yarn, attached to the leader above a nymph or other wet fly.

Strip v. Retrieval of the fly line with the hand not holding the fly rod.

Structure n. Large objects in a stream or lake, such as big rocks, trees, dock pilings, etc., around which fish will stay.

Surgeon's Knot n. An easy knot to tie, it is used to attach tippet material to the end of a leader.

Tail Out n. A location in a stream found at the end of a pool, where it again becomes shallow, fast-moving water over a rocky or sandy bottom.

Tailwaters n. A river that's fed from the bottom of a dam.

Terrestrial n. A fly tied to imitate an insect that was not born in the water, such as a grasshopper, cricket, ant, or beetle.

Tippet Material n. Very thin, monofilament material added to the end of a leader to extend the length or to rebuild the leader after some of the tippet section has been used up tying knots or broken off in fishing.

Trout n. A member of the Salmonids family of fish that are major targets for fly fishers.

Wader Belt n. A stretchable belt worn around the waist of a pair of waders, intended to keep the water out of waders should the wearer slip and fall into the water.

Weight n. An accepted system of measuring fly line size. Fly lines come in Weights from 1 (the lightest) to 15 (the heaviest). Not necessarily a function of line strength, it is determined by the actual weight of the first 30 feet of line.

Weight Forward adj. Used to describe a fly line designed with more weight toward the front of the fly line to assist in casting.

Wet Fly n. A fly fished below, or in the surface film of water.

Wild adj. A term applied to fish that were born in the waters in which they are found, as opposed to fish that were raised in a hatchery and stocked into their current waters.

Woolly Bugger n. A type of wet fly tied to imitate nothing in particular, but rather to give the impression of a number of underwater food items a fish may be interested in.

"X" Ratings n. A system of describing the approximate thickness of leaders and tippet material. The X Rating system runs from 010X (equaling .021 diameter at the tippet = very large) down to 7X (equaling .004 diameter at the tippet = smaller than a human hair).

Definitions from The Easy Field Guide to Fly-Fishing Terms & Tips *by David Phares. For the complete list of terms, tips and some humor send $2.00 to:Primer Publishers 5738 North Central Avenue Phoenix, Arizona 85012*

Other
No Nonsense Guides

Bob Zeller's No Nonsense Business Traveler's Guide To Fly Fishing The Western States

This seasoned road warrior reveals where one can fly fish within a two hour drive from every major airport in thirteen western states.
ISBN #1-892469-01-4

Traveling on business (or for some other reason)? Turn drudgery into a fun fly fishing outing. Here's how to pack, what to tell the boss, and what to expect. Lots of detailed, two colored maps show where to go and how to get there.

With to-the-point facts and humor Bob's 30 years of fly fishing-while-on-the-road are your guide to exploring the outdoors, not just a hotel lobby or airport lounge.

Glenn Tinnin's No Nonsense Guide To Fly Fishing In Arizona

Black River, Lees Ferry, Chevelon, Christmas Tree, Powell, and Lee Valley lakes, The Little Colorado River, Oak Creek and more!
ISBN #1-892469-02-2

If visiting the many scenic wonders of the Grand Canyon State, or moving there, bring your rod and this guide! Glenn Tinnin, outfitter at The Complete Fly Fisher in Scottsdale has explored Arizona's fly fishing waters for over 20 years. He explains where to go and how to fly fish mountain streams, lakes, bass waters, reservoirs and nearby saltwater fly fishing in Mexico.

Dave Stanley's No Nonsense Guide To Fly Fishing In Nevada

The Truckee, Walker, Carson, Eagle, Davis, Ruby, mountain lakes and more.
ISBN #0-9637256-2-9

Mr. Stanley is recognized nationwide as the most knowledgeable fly fisher and outdoorsman in the state of Nevada. He also travels throughout the west and other warm climes where he leads fly fishing excursions. He owns and operates the Reno Fly Shop and River Outfitters in Truckee.

The guide's talented coauthor, Jeff Cavender, is a Nevada native. Jeff teaches fly casting and tying. He's taught and guided all over Nevada and California during the past 30 + years. He also edits fly fishing guidebooks.

A Woman's No Nonsense Guide To Fly Fishing Favorite Waters

Compiled and edited by Yvonne Graham
A First In Fly Fishing Guidebooks!
ISBN #1-892469-03-0

Forty five of the top woman fly fishing experts reveal their favorite waters. From scenic spring creeks in the East, big trout waters in the Rockies to exciting Baja saltwater: all described from the distinctive female perspective.

A major donation from each printing will go to Casting For Recovery, a non-profit organization that assists women who are in various stages of recovery from breast cancer.

A few of the female fly fishing "Who's Who" authorities, guides, writers and tiers who are contributors: Maggie Merriman, Joan Wulff, Mina Hemingway, Yvonne Graham, Fanny Krieger, Sister Mary Anne Corley "The Tying Nun", Jodi Pate, Margot Page, Lisa Cutter, Wanda Taylor, Cecelia Kleinkauf, Page Rogers, Joan Stoliar, Kate Howe, Mallory Burton, Mary Deete Clark and many more.

Unique reasons to go fly fishing, regional flies and special places to just "be where you are." Anyone who fishes the fly will want to find out about these favorite home waters. Lots of detailed maps, illustrations and "how to get there" information.

Some of the Woman's Favorite waters include The S. Platte River, CO, The Madison River, MT, Sweet Spring Creek, VA, Denali River, AK, Big Pine Creek, CA, Hiwassee River, TN, Hilton Head Island, SC, Crooked River, OR, Stellaku River, BC, Bullhead Creek, NC, Cape Cod & Martha's Vineyard, MA, The Truckee River, CA, Yellowstone River, MT, East Cape, Baja, New York Harbor, NY, Beaverkill River, NY, And Many More!

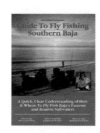

Gary Graham's No Nonsense Guide To Fly Fishing Southern Baja

With this book you can fly to Baja, rent a car and go out on your own and find exciting saltwater fly fishing!
ISBN #1-892469-00-6

Mexico's Baja Peninsula is now one of the premier destinations for saltwater fly anglers. Here's the latest and best information from Baja fly fishing authority, Gary Graham. This Orvis endorsed guide has over 20 years of Baja fishing experience. He operates *Baja on the Fly*, a top guiding operation located in Baja's famed "East Cape" region.

Bill Mason's No Nonsense Guide To
Fly Fishing In Idaho

The Henry's Fork, Salmon, Snake and Silver Creek plus 24 other waters.
ISBN #0-9637256-1-0

Mr. Mason penned the first fly fishing guidebook to Idaho in 1994. It was updated in 1996 and showcases Bill's 30 plus years of Idaho fly fishing experience.

Bill helped build a major outfitting operation at the Henry's Fork and helped open the first fly shop in Boise. In Sun Valley he developed the first fly fishing school and guiding program at Snug Fly Fishing. Bill eventually purchased the shop, renaming it Bill Mason Sun Valley Outfitters.

Jackson Streit's No Nonsense Guide To
Fly Fishing In Colorado

The Colorado, Rio Grande, Platte, Gunnison, Mountain lakes and more.
ISBN #0-9637256-4-5

Mr. Streit fly fished Colorado for over 28 years and condensed this experience into a guidebook, published in 1995 and updated, improved and reprinted in 1997.

Jackson started the first guide service in the Breckenridge area and in 1985 he opened the region's first fly shop, The Mountain Angler, which he owns and manages.

Look for new No Nonsense fly fishing guides to other important regions!

Ken Hanley's No Nonsense Guide To
Fly Fishing In Northern California

The "Sac", Hat Creek, Russian River, reservoirs, saltwater and bass on a fly.
ISBN #0-9637256-5-3

Mr. Hanley has fly fished nearly every water in N. California. While traveling the world and leading adventure expeditions he's caught over 50 species of gamefish. He's also written much on the subject including five other books. Ken also writes outdoor related pieces for a variety of publications.

Terry Barron's No Nonsense Guide To
Fly Fishing Pyramid Lake

The Gem of the Desert is full of huge Lahontan Cutthroat trout.
ISBN #0-9637256-3-7

Mr. Barron is the Reno-area and Pyramid Lake fly fishing guru. He helped establish the Truckee River Fly Fishers Club and ties and works for the Reno Fly Shop.

Terry has recorded the pertinent information to fly fish the most outstanding trophy cutthroat fishery in the U.S. Where else can you get tired of catching 18-25" trout?

Harry Teel's No Nonsense Guide To
Fly Fishing In Central & Southeastern Oregon

The Metolius, Deschutes, McKenzie, Owyhee, John Day and 35 other waters.
ISBN #0-9637256-9-6

Mr. Teel combined his 60 years of fly fishing into the first No Nonsense fly fishing guide. It was published in 1993 and updated, expanded and improved in 1998 by Jeff Perin. Jeff owns and operates the Fly Fisher's Place, the premier fly shop in Sisters, Oregon originally started by Mr. Teel.

Where No Nonsense Guides Come From

No Nonsense guidebooks give you a quick, clear, understanding of the essential information needed to fly fish a region's most outstanding waters. The authors are highly experienced and qualified local fly fishers. Maps are tidy versions of their sketches.

These guides are produced by the fly fishers, their friends, and spouses of fly fishers, at David Communications. The publisher is located in the tiny Western town of Sisters, Oregon, just a few miles from the Metolius River.

All who produce No Nonsense guides believe in providing top quality products at a reasonable price. We also believe all information should be verified. We never hesitate to go out, fly rod in hand, to verify the facts and figures that appear in the pages of these guides. The staff is committed to this research. It's dirty work, but we're glad to do it for you.

The layout, illustrations and maps in these books are the work of Pete Chadwell. As a fly fisherman, Pete is more than happy to apply his considerable drawing talents to things that live and float in and on water. His detailed maps are a testimony to his desire for accuracy and to get out and fly fish new waters.

No Nonsense fly fishing guides are edited by two and an amateur. Cavender, casting instructor, guide and author edits and writes fly fishing articles, books and guides. David Banks did the minor and amateur editing.

Weigh Your Catch With A Tape Measure

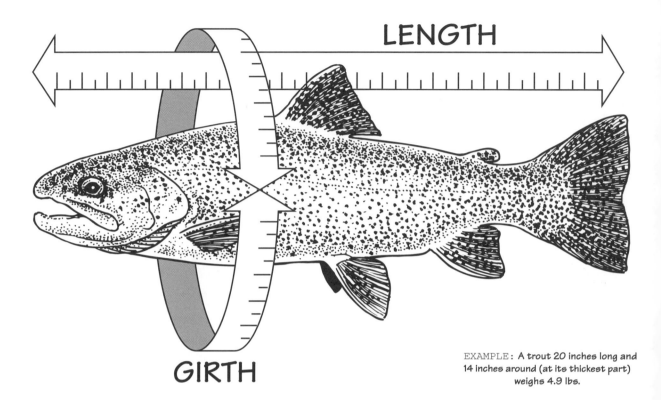

LENGTH

GIRTH

EXAMPLE: A trout 20 inches long and 14 inches around (at its thickest part) weighs 4.9 lbs.

LENGTH (inches)
Tip of nose to notch at the center of tail.

GIRTH (inches)	0	10	12	14	16	18	20	22	24	26	28	30
8		.8	1.0	1.1	1.3	1.4	1.6	1.8	1.9	2.1	2.2	2.4
10		1.3	1.5	1.8	2.0	2.3	2.5	2.8	3.0	3.3	3.5	3.8
12		1.8	2.2	2.5	2.9	3.2	3.6	4.0	4.3	4.7	5.0	5.4
14		2.5	2.9	3.4	3.9	4.4	4.9	5.4	5.9	6.4	6.9	7.4
16		3.2	3.8	4.5	5.1	5.8	6.4	7.0	7.7	8.3	9.0	9.6
18		4.1	4.9	5.7	6.5	7.3	8.1	8.9	9.7	10.5	11.3	12.2
20		5.0	6.0	7.0	8.0	9.0	10.0	11.0	12.0	13.0	14.0	15.0

Courtesy of Ralph & Lisa Cutter's California School of Flyfishing • P.O. Box 8212 • Truckee, CA 96162 • 1-800-58-TROUT

Why is the fish "Old Walter" smiling? Because Taylor Streit practices catch & release.

Photo: Garrett Vene Klasen

Notes on Fly Fishing in New Mexico

Notes on Fly Fishing in New Mexico

STATE OF NEW MEXICO
MAJOR HIGHWAY NETWORK

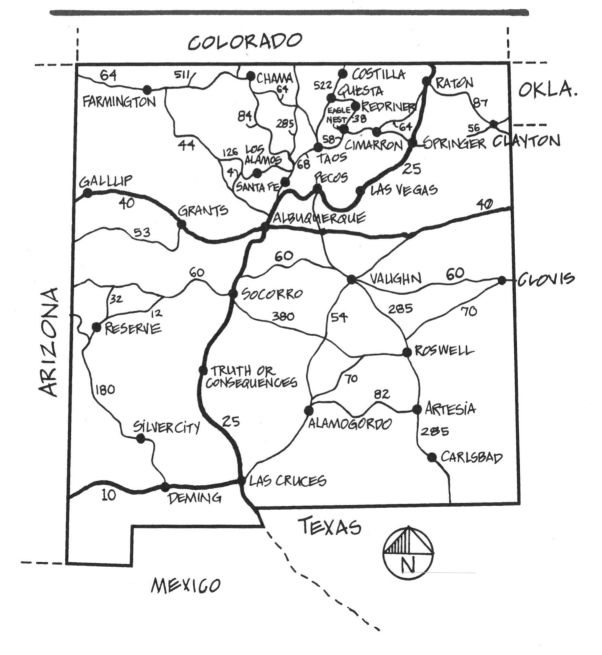